DUDLEY PUBLIC LIBRARIES

The loan of this book may be renewed if not required by other
readers, by contacting the library from which it was borrowed.

TOMMY COOPER'S
SECRET JOKE FILES

AB
CD
EF
GH
IJ
KL
MN
OP
QR
ST
UV
WX
YZ

for Terry & Lynne Wright

CONTENTS

CONTENTS

UNDER THE WEATH
SWIMMING POOL
THOUGHT IV
STAGGING
STRONG MR STORIES
SINGING BIT
TRAIN
TRAFFIC
TOYS
SHORT COMEDY
REMARKS OVERHEARD ON PLANES
RELIGIO RECORD
PSYCHIATRIST
RELIGION
PROPERTY TAS
PERFUME JOKE PARTIES
ONE LINERS
NIGHT CLUBS
NEIGHBOUR
LANDLADIES
PERSONAL
INSURANCE
KARATE
KN
HOTELS
HONEST HOLIDAYS
HOLLYWOOD
HOLIDA
HUMOROUS
HEN PECKED HUSBAND MONO.
HECKLER SQUELCHERS
HEALTH MONOLOGUE
HEALTH
FAMILY
FURNISHING
FOOD
FAMOUS PEO
FAITH, HOPE CHARITY
EXERCISE
DRUNKS
DRINK
DRINKS
DRINK
DANCING
CRUISE
HONESTY
DIETING
DENTIST
COURTSHIP
CRIME
COUNTRYSI
COOKING
COMEDY SONG
CIRCL
CHILDREN
CHILDHOOD
CARS
CARS
CAMERAS
BOWLING
BOOKS
BEAUTY
BATHIN
BASEBALL
BAR
BARBERS
BANQUETS
BALLET
BAB SITT
RMY
APARTMENTS
ANNOYANCE
ANNIVERSARY
ANIMALS
AGENTS

'Saving for Comedy's Rainy Day ... '

An introduction by John Fisher

It was no surprise to anyone who understood the dedication and attention to detail required by the master magician that there should be method in the madness of the most hysterical hocus-pocus man of all time. To create the continual illusion of incompetence in such a specialised area required an adroitness and split-second precision that rivalled the skills of any of the members of the 'now-you-see-it' brigade of which Tommy Cooper was both proud to be a member and yet astute enough to ridicule for his own greater popularity. But the laughter generated by his (sometimes) failed conjuring tricks was only half of the matter. Complementing his escapades with the bottle and the glass and the egg and the bag was a string of seemingly inconsequential patter ostensibly justified purely by the surrealism of its placing. One-liners, shaggy dog stories, visual puns and schoolboy howlers would be addressed to the audience with the seeming innocence and abandon with which he handled scarves, playing cards and all the other trademarks of the magician's trade. Cooper first responded to the sound of an audience's laughter at an early age when the milk that was supposed to stay in the upturned bottle cascaded to the floor of the shipyard canteen where he worked for part of his teenage years. From that moment the magic he targeted for his act was chosen for its comedy potential. As he progressed in the business, it was inevitable that he would need to segue into something approaching stand-up comedy if he did not wish to be pigeonholed on the cabaret and variety circuits as a mere speciality act. Hidden away in the innermost recesses of his Chiswick home at the time of his death was a secret hoard of jokes and gags that testified how important this consideration would prove to his success.

In a previous volume, 'The Tommy Cooper Joke Book,' I have explained his debt in this regard to the doyen of British stand-up comedians, Max Miller, as well as to his early reliance on the long series of soft-covered joke books compiled by the American gagster Robert Orben, which for a couple of decades winged their way across the Atlantic to the counters of the London magical depots where Cooper bought his tricks. Orben had been a magician and many of his lines were devised with their relevance to a particular piece of apparatus in mind. It was said that if for your fourteen shillings you used merely one joke out of the many included in the average forty or so pages, you got your money's worth. Cooper must have gained more value from them than anyone else. In time, his increased stature and earning power enabled him – and the television companies that employed him – to pay for custom-scripted material, from writers like Eddie Bayliss, Val Andrews and Freddie Sadler. But it is an accepted fact that no comedian feels he ever has enough material and Tommy was more voracious than most. On his first trip to America in 1954 he became familiar with the work of Billy Glason, an ex-vaudevillian who in his inevitable spare time on tour had compiled an index of every joke he ever heard on stage and every gag he was ever told off it. Upon retirement he set to and ordered everything he had gathered and much else besides into a series of home-produced publications obtainable only through limited subscription and at high prices. Ed Sullivan, Johnny Carson and Bob Hope all availed themselves of his service. Cooper was lucky to become his sole British client and in the process found himself the unofficial archivist in the UK for everything Billy produced.

Dominating this pile of material produced on flimsy typing paper in a pre-Xerox age were the twenty-six parts of the 'Fun-Master Encyclopaedia of Classified Gags.' The work was advertised at three thousand dollars, although Tommy was able to acquire the same for a knockdown price of nine hundred. Its high cost was determined by the strictly limited edition. How many copies can you achieve with a typewriter and carbon paper? Cooper's, which must have been at the end of the run, are only just legible, the thinnest paper being used *'to make it possible to make as many carbon copies as we can!'* To make the print legible, each transparent wafer-thin page is interleaved with a heavier blank white sheet! Before long Tommy added in similar format to his shelves Glason's five-volume 'Book of Blackouts,' the nine sections of his 'Comedy and Emcee Lecture Book,' as well as the 'Humor-Dor for Emcees and Comedians.' Glason eventually progressed to mimeographing techniques and was able to circulate more of the same to a much wider clientele on a monthly basis in a gag-sheet called simply 'The Comedian.' Tommy signed up for this too, as he did for rival periodic publications like Art Paul's 'Punch Lines' and Eddie Gay's 'Gay's Gags.' Further material that sneaked its way into his files on a less regular basis comprised joke sheets by Pinkie DuFort and Vince Healy, vaudevillians all.

Upon Tommy's death this all amounted to a pile of paper almost twice as tall as the fez-capped giant himself. It is hard to believe that he ever read it all or needed much of it. But he did, on both counts. On the latter point, it was less a joke library for reference than an archive as security blanket. Every comedian lives in dread of the day when that tried and tested line fails to raise a laugh, tantamount to feeling the hand on your shoulder of the great joke-master in the sky calling in your comedy dues. But with a million or more gags to choose from, Cooper assumed he could sleep more soundly at night. That is, if he managed to get much sleep – he was determined to get his money's worth and made sure he read every joke from crumpled front cover to staple-snagged back page. He missed nothing and it is an indication of his seriousness to the joke that he was determined to take full advantage in this way over his rivals on the British comedy scene. What makes these aging reams so fascinating now is the process of selection and rehearsal they reveal. And it is here that we see the method in his madness again.

This book sets out to share with the reader the procedure Cooper employed in adapting this vast store of comedy for his own ends. It is likely that with the exception of the more risqué material reserved for stag events every single joke in these pages figured in his act at some stage, although obviously only a small percentage of them graduated to become the beloved almost-clichéd Cooper one-liners and shaggy dog tales that now contribute so vividly to his legend. He only needed so many of either, but every stage or cabaret performance allowed him a tiny oasis of experimentation in which he vowed to try out a new gag or two. If the casualty rate was high, it is only because of the power of the tried and tested nature of his core material.

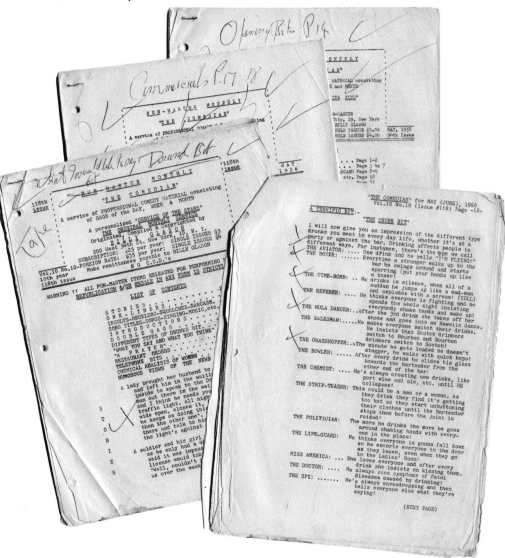

As he read each page, he marked the jokes that appealed with a tick. Sometimes he scrawled a specific reference or instruction on the front page of a joke bulletin. The two most frequent commands were 'Type' and 'Tape.'

MASTER MONTHLY

E   COMEDIAN"

PROFESSIONAL COMEDY MATERIAL
GAGS of the DAY-WEEK-MONTH

zed "SERVICE OF THE STARS"
INAL   MONTHLY   SERVICE"
                    righted by

ISSUE #150
6th issue
13th year

Typed

GAY'S GAGS
242 West 72nd St.
New York 23, N.Y.

PER YEAR   MARCH 1961   ISSUE N

TERIAL WRITTEN BY EDDIE GAY

Tape

f my left foot---that's why I keep i
y swing---later he fo
n having trouble with
Khrushchev.....My ho
ral person---except w
wo handicap---my slic
y tough lies I thought
er and my last was a te
course than there were
ly I've been getting
s after he gets in offi
were faster than Suera

Tape

THE ENTERTAINER
242 West 72nd Street
New York City
SU 7-4068

thly $10 per year   March 1959   Issue No. 3

ORIGINAL MATERIAL WRITTEN BY EDDIE GAY

DAY

20

FUN-MASTER
(Title Reg. U. S. Patent Office)
GAG FILE No. 20
Compiled by Billy Glason

Tape

STORIES

lyer came to America for a visit on a ve
d a friend about America's
of our cou

MONTHLY

MEDIAN"

L COMEDY MATERIAL
e DA Y-WEEK-MONTH

OF THE STARS"
Y   SERVICE"
opyrighted by
SON
k City, 19, N.Y.
GLE ISSUES $3
GLE ISSUES $4
U.S. FUNDS)
GLASON

ISSUE #149
5th issue
13th year

Typed

I S S U E
#149

OR PERFORMING RIGHTS ONLY

M O N T H L Y

COMEDIAN"

SIONAL COMEDY MATERIAL consisting
e DAY, WEEK and MONTH

ished   by
GLASON'S FUN-MASTER
n Street, New York City, 19, New York
mittances payable to BILLY GLASON
SCRIPTION: $15 pr year

Typed

A P R I L
1 9 5 5

LIST OF CONTENTS

AIES.........
- LINE

#2

FUN-MASTER GAG FILE #24
(Title Reg. U. S. Patent Office)
Compiled by Billy Glason

for a ride on his new motorcycle. After they had gone a few
ked it.   "Shure and it's fine", said Mike, "But the
by the side of the road and said: "Turn your
that shud protect your chest".   They we
truck. When the constable arrived
both dead.   This man here w
ll I twisted his neck

age 1-
4-1
14
14
15
15

11

'Tape' constituted a reminder for the designated material to be rehearsed for his own experimentation into a reel-to-reel machine. 'Type' specified that the marked gags were destined for transcribing onto a sheet of A4 for eventual insertion into an elaborate A – Z index categorised by joke topic. This index also accommodated his choices from the bulkier volumes. Sometimes a subject would be assigned two sub-categories, marked 'P' and '1-L' accordingly. 'P' stood for Personal and '1-L' for One-liner. Thus under A for Army we find

ARMY   "PERSONAL"

In the last war I fought and fought--but I had to go anyway.

in the first group and

ARMY   ONE-LINERS

If you wanna stay outta the Army   "JOIN THE NAVY".

in the latter.

Likewise 'H' for Health yields

HEALTH   "PERSONAL"

I'm recovering from a cold---I'm so full of penicillin, that if I sneeze, I'll cure someone.

as well as

HEALTH   ONE-LINERS

The best way to avoid a cold is to drink a lot of water. You never saw a FISH with a cold.

Once Tommy had inserted the joke in the A-Z file, another stroke of his ballpoint converted his original tick into a cross. In time he compiled an extraordinarily large and somewhat cumbersome system. At some stage he decided to upgrade the material by adding tabs that enabled him to read and access the categories more clearly. The task was never completed with the result that the full accumulation of material remains divided arbitrarily into two large sections, one with tabs and one with tabs pending. He also experimented for a while with typing individual gags on more conventional index cards, a process that surprisingly soon lost favour given the more compact nature of the format.

Tommy never claimed an academic approach to the business of laughter in the way that some of his contemporaries were perceived. The brilliant Ken Dodd has been referred to as the slide-rule comic and may possibly have every book on laughter and its theory on his shelves. Bob Monkhouse could not have been far behind as a bibliophile and as he toured from show to show clung to two flight cases containing his scrupulously hand-written and illustrated joke books as if they were first folios of Shakespeare. Today the originality of the likes of Jimmy Carr, Harry Hill and Tim Vine owes much to an intellectual exercise in which words and concepts, logic and meaning collide with each other until the joke emerges fully formed. But, however the joke is achieved, its viability must always come down to a basic gut reaction. Cooper knew what would work for him. 'If it's funny, it's funny,' was a line he repeated often. And as he perused line after line he looked for the elements that spelt 'funny' to him – the play on words that rendered the obvious surprising, the visual quality that turned a joke into a cartoon of the imagination, the lateral thought that shed a quirky light on reality. He once confided, 'You have to have such innocent faith in a joke that the audience just has to laugh.' His words reinforce the fact that the selection procedure was no slapdash affair.

To many, the painstaking process that Tommy adopted will appear out of step with the idiosyncrasies of his stage character, but as one investigates the results of his efforts it is reassuring to discover instances where the old dysfunctional persona appears to shine through. 'A' for Animals, for Army and for Art speak for themselves, but then one encounters a category 'A for Actor-Cannons.' There cannot be many gags that feature both thespians and heavy artillery, but here we find one with a category all to itself, although one does wonder when and where he would have needed such a particular specimen. Its specification may well mean it was lost for all time as far as he was concerned. Now if he had filed it under 'A' for Actor or 'C' for Cannon…? For the record, here it is:

Actor - Cannons.

An actor got a job to fill in for a part and had to leave for Boston where the show was playing. All he had was one line "HARK! I HEAR THE CANNONS ROAR!" All day long he rehearsed the line, wherever he was, whether he was walking, eating or riding in the subway. All he kept repeating was "HARK! I HEAR THE CANNONS ROAR!" He finally got on the train to Boston and all the way he kept drumming the line into his head "HARK! I HEAR THE CANNONS ROAR". When he got to the theatre they were waiting for him. The show had already begun. He got dressed and on the stage he went, running the line through his head. All of a sudden came the time for his line and when the cannons went BOOM! he yelled "WHAT THE HELL WAS THAT?"

Other categories suggest a man struggling with a thesaurus. Why 'I' for Ignition and not simply 'Hot,' 'Heat' or 'Burning'? 'Well Dressed' seems a strange heading for a stray gag that was tailor-made (no pun intended)

WELL DRESSED

In a Nudist Colony there was one fellow wearing a
long beard and when he was asked what the idea of the
long beard was, he said "Well, SOMEONE'S gotta go out for
coffee!"

for 'N for Nudist' or even 'C for Clothes,' where he has a joke where the phrase 'well dressed' itself motivates the gag. 'Private Purposes' is a somewhat limiting category for a joke that might have been more easily found under 'P for Pub' or 'S for Sailor':

PRIVATE PURPOSES

Two sailors retired from the Navy and decided to
pool their savings and buy a saloon in a small town
and they started to paint it up and give it a real
good fixing inside and out. A few days later
after all the repairs were made, there STILL wasn't
any sign of an opening. One day a crowd began to
gather around the front and started yelling "HEY YOU
GUYS, WHEN ARE YA GONNA OPEN UP THIS JOINT?" One of
the sailors stuck his head out of the door and yelled
back "What dya mean, OPEN UP? Are you guys NUTS?
We ain't GONNA open up, we bought this joint for
OURSELVES!"

Indeed, there was often no rhyme nor reason why a joke should be filed one way or another. He had a category for 'Interior Decorator.' The lone joke filed here could as easily have been placed under 'Psychiatrist,' while many of the gags filed under the latter could have found refuge under other categories.

Interior decorator - Woman seeking advice

A woman went to an interior decorator and was having
a tough time getting what she wanted and finally
confessed to the Decorator that her husband think's
he's a BEAR. The Decorator said "A BEAR? Why don't
you go to a psychiatrist?" and she said "Do you think
HE can tell me what colour scheme to use in a CAVE?"

Most of the so-called 'R for Risqué' material is harmless enough, although a few other categories stretch the imagination in the light of Cooper's commitment to clean comedy: 'F' for Family Planning, 'L' for Love Bites.

He certainly would never have used these jokes for mainstream shows, innocent though they seem now.

FAMILY PLANNING!!

Once there was a couple who had 18 children. One day the husband said to his wife "No more kids. If you ever tell me you're gonna have another baby, I'll shoot myself!" A year later, the wife said "Darling, I got news for you. We're gonna have another baby", so the husband grabbed his gun, went into the bathroom and put the gun to his head. Suddenly he stopped and said "What am I doing? I may be killing an innocent man.'"

LOVE BITES

A man awakened by his wife's crying, so he put the light on and went over to her side of the bed and asked her why she was crying. She said "You never kiss me goodnight anymore and I'm beginning to think you don't love me". He said, "Don't be silly, SURE I love ya" and he bent over and gave her a peck and said "NOW SHUT UP!" and around to his side of the bed he went and put the light out and went to sleep. She began to whimper again and woke him up. He said "NOW what's the matter with you?" She said "You call that a kiss? Some men bite their wives on the ear and the neck and all I get from you is a lousy peck". All of a sudden there was a terrific crash. His wife jumped up and yelled "What happened?" He said "You and your crazy ideas, I WAS LOOKING FOR MY TEETH!"

There is the inevitable emphasis (over-emphasis?) on wives (both generic and his own), members of the medical profession (medical, surgical and psychiatric), and members of the animal kingdom, not least dogs. He loved rambling animal stories with a delayed punch line. 'Shaggy dog' signifies the genre, although it usually featured beasts of larger size and fiercer disposition. Significantly he assigned the word 'Jungley!!' to same – the adjectival form and exclamation marks spelling out his special enthusiasm. On stage it was often in this category that he revealed his great gift for embellishing the material at his disposal. A typical 'shaggy dog' story featured the King of the Jungle. He originally typed it out as he found it in the American source:

<u>JUNGLEY!!</u> - Big LION feeling insecure.

A big lion was suffering from a feeling of insecurity, and as he roared through the jungle one day he had this chip on his shoulder. Every animal he came across he'd stop them and say "Who is the King of Beasts?" and he was told that HE was. Finally he bumped into a mean, nasty-tempered elephant so he stopped him and said "Hey Jumbo, who is the King of Beasts?" so the elephant grabbed the lion with his trunk, tossed him into the air half a dozen times and then slammed him against a big tree. The lion picked himself up and said "Okay, but just because you don't know the ANSWER, you don't have to get SORE about it!"

When I wrote *Always Leave Them Laughing*, my biography of the comedian, I set myself the task of transcribing the sequence exactly as it sounded and appeared in his act:

You know – the king of the jungle – the lion. And one day he woke up – he had a very bad temper – and he said to himself, 'I'm just going outside now and teach them all who's king of the jungle. Just to teach them.' So he gets up and he goes, 'Grrrrrr.' He was really mad, you know what I mean? 'Grrrrrr.' And he saw a little chimp and he said, 'You! Who's the king of the jungle?' And he said, 'You. You're the king of the jungle.' 'Well that's alright then. Alright.' And he walked along a bit more and he came across a laughing hyena and he said, 'Hey you, laughing boy.' And he went, 'Hah hah, hah hah hah. Hah hah, hah hah hah!' He said, 'Who's the king of the jungle?' 'Ooh, aah aah hah, ooh ooh aah, you are, you are.' So he walked on a little bit further and right at the very end was an elephant and a gorilla talking. And this gorilla looked at the elephant and he said, 'Here he comes, Jumbo. He's gonna do that "king of the jungle" bit again. He always does it.' He said, 'I'm not gonna stand it any more. I'm gonna leave you.' And he went up a tree. He said, 'I'll give you a trunk call later.' Hah hah hah! So he went up to this elephant and he said, 'Hey you. I'm talking to you, big ears.' He said, 'Who's the king of the jungle?' And this elephant got his trunk and wrapped it right round him and threw him up in the air and as he was up in the air coming down he was going, 'Who's the king of the jungle? Who's the king of the jungle?' And he hit the ground hard. And he picked him up again and he threw him against the tree and he threw him against the other tree. Then the other one. Then the other one. Then the other one. And he sank to the ground like that. It may have been like that. No. It was like that. And the lion said to the elephant, 'Look, there's no good getting mad just because you don't know the answer!'

It is impossible to convey on the page the effect Cooper achieved as he enhanced the telling of the story with mime, burlesque, audience acknowledgement and sheer physical effort. No wonder distinguished thespians like Hopkins, Gambon and Callow have such a high regard for him. However, he never became greedy with the principle. He was equally a master at simplification and concision, able to hone and perfect a joke until it was so streamlined it just *had to* connect with the audience.

What appeared in the Fun-Master archive as

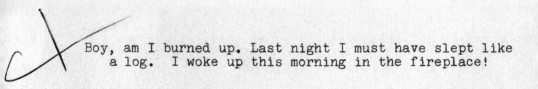

Boy, am I burned up. Last night I must have slept like a log. I woke up this morning in the fireplace!

became

Last night I slept like a log. I woke up in the fireplace.

Similarly

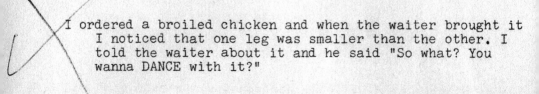

I ordered a broiled chicken and when the waiter brought it I noticed that one leg was smaller than the other. I told the waiter about it and he said "So what? You wanna DANCE with it?"

became

I said, 'Waiter, this chicken's got one leg shorter than the other.' He said, 'What do you want to do? Eat it or dance with it?'

Since the wealth of the material at Cooper's disposal in this way originated in the United States, it was not surprising that occasionally a major cultural shift would be called for. Take, for example,

```
A Beatnik in Greenwich Village rigged up a do-it-yourself
   charcoal grill on his fire-escape and put a chicken
   on it to broil, when he heard one of his Beatnik
   pals yell up "Hey Dad, I don t wanna bug ya, but
   your music box has stopped and your monkey is on
   fire!"
```

The text is almost unrecognisable as the classic Cooper gem it became. Translated to London suburbia and transplanted to his act the joke became transformed as follows.

There's a guy having a barbecue in his front garden. He's turning the spit like this and the flames are getting higher and higher – higher and higher – and he's singing, 'O sole mio … O sole mio, farewell.' And the flames are getting higher and higher and this drunk walks by and says, 'Your singing's alright, but your monkey's on fire!'

He had to be ever alert to the need for Anglicisation, although he was happy to include in his index categories for quintessentially American subjects like Thanksgiving, Drug Store, Dude Ranch, Democrat, Miami (as a holiday destination) - topics he knew he could always work around to his own more localised ends. As if to tell us that the period when he was active in this regard bridged the mid-fifties to the early seventies, he even compiled his own cache of jokes appertaining to the Brain Drain, the Space Race, the

Cold War and Vietnam, even though topicality was never a concern of Cooper's humour, a stance that provides one of the reasons why his spoken comedy still works today. However, to maintain the colour of the original, no effort has been made in this volume to update references to dance crazes, sex symbols or political scapegoats of the time where their meaning will still be understood. In some cases today's reality has rendered yesterday's jokes less funny than they might have been when first devised. The unintended presentiment makes them no less interesting and a few examples have been included for curiosity's sake, as with

PARKING

The parking situation is still so tough that some guys are carrying bicycles in their cars to get to and from parking places.'

and

BUSINESS

I've just made a terrific deal. I bought up all the heat in town and I'm storing it away till the WINTER.'
(A GOOD SUMMER GAG)

Only very occasionally would a joke be credited in the joke bulletins to its original American practitioner, but on those occasions Cooper carried over the credit, with the result that comedy legends like Fred Allen, Jack Benny, Milton Berle, Buddy Hackett and Henny Youngman make cameo appearances in the pages that follow.

It is possible in the space available to feature only a fraction of the material Cooper set in store for comedy's rainy day. For the sake of simplicity, I have discarded his occasional distinction between 'P' and '1-L' material. That speaks for itself on the printed page. In some cases I have re-categorised jokes to make the text more user-friendly and even added new categories, as, for example, with 'D for Dog,' where previously all the 'Dog' jokes were listed under 'A for Animal.' Tommy also sometimes marked gags on the joke sheets that he never got around to entering in his A-Z index. Some of them have now found their intended destination. I have also taken the liberty of sometimes rephrasing a joke if the voice in my head has told me that doing so would have better suited his delivery. My own selection process has been helped – and made all the more enjoyable – by the simple device of reading through his files with that unmistakable voice in one's ears, a sound he himself likened to 'combing a wire-haired terrier against the grain'! For maximum pleasure readers are asked to follow the same course.

'Tommy Cooper's Secret Joke Files' are being published in what would have been the year of his ninetieth birthday, twenty-seven years after his death on live television on 15 April 1984. Tucked away in the pages that follow is a joke that has an especially poignant subtext in that respect:

<u>TV</u>

```
I always had trouble getting on TV.  I even offered
to kill myself on TV.  It would be a real first!
```

He never meant it that way, of course, just as he never meant to leave us at the moment he did with so many jokes untold and so many tricks still to be tried. Since his death both his persona and his material have passed into the stuff of folklore to an extent that has eluded his comedy contemporaries. He would never have envisaged it that way. By his own modest interpretation he saw himself as a comparative amateur up against the likes of Benny Hill, Frankie Howerd and Morecambe & Wise and always swore they were far funnier than he was. To ensure he kept up with them he had to work hard and, figuratively speaking, stay on his toes. As this is being written, a poll has just been published in which Cooper has been credited with no less than thirteen of the top fifty jokes of all time, more than any other comedian, with five in the top ten alone and poll position to boot. The following pages will enable the reader to look over Tommy's shoulder as he stared much of his material in the face for the first hard time and confronted the challenge of staying in the comedy race, oblivious of the fact that in another lifetime he would prove to be the undisputed winner by miles.

A is for Army

Absent-Minded

I used to be very absent-minded, so one night I took a piece of paper and wrote on it, 'Shirt in the wardrobe ... tie on the tie rack ... trousers on the chair ... shoes and socks on the floor' ... and then I went to sleep. The next morning when I got up everything was where it should have been. My shoes and socks were on the floor, my trousers were on the chair, my tie was on the tie rack and my shirt was in the wardrobe. Then I looked at the bed and I wasn't there!

Actor-Cannons

See Introduction: page 10

After-Dinner Speaking

He's a great after-dinner speaker. He's always on the phone when the waiter brings the bill!

How to make a successful speech: Get up! Speak up! Shut up! Sit down!

When I came here today I had a beautiful speech all prepared and only God and I knew what I was going to say. Now I can't find it and God only knows!

I'm always nervous before getting up to make a speech, but as soon as I hear my own voice, I'm reassured!

The greatest after-dinner speech of them all is 'Put it all on one bill and don't hand it to me!'

One way to shorten after-dinner speeches would be to have them before dinner!

Today we're pleased to have as a speaker a man who has a train to catch in fifteen minutes!

Agents

If you want to get on in show business, you've got to have an agent.
In fact, I've got two ... they're double agents!

My agent is a great bloke. Well, without him I wouldn't be working here
today ... I'd have retired ten years ago!

Alarm Clock

A woman rushed into the hospital with her little boy and said, 'Doctor,
my little boy has swallowed an alarm clock.' He said, 'An alarm clock?
Does it bother him?' She said, 'It doesn't bother him, but it bothers me.'
He said, 'Why?' She said, 'Well, every time I go to wind it up, he bites
my finger.'

Alphabet

My little boy learnt the alphabet. I said, 'What comes after A?' He said,
'All the rest of them!'

Animals

A fellow kept his pet mice in the top drawer of his dresser and kept some
cheese in the bottom drawer. His friend said, 'How do you stop the mice
from getting at the cheese?' He said, 'Oh, in the middle drawer I keep
my cat.'

One day I was drinking some milk and a cow fell on me!

Two sheep were together in the meadow when one of them went, 'Baa-aa.'
The other sheep went, 'Moo-oo.' The first one said, 'Moo? What's this
"Moo" bit?' and the second one said, 'I'm taking up a foreign language!'

A fellow saw a man coming towards him with an animal on his shoulder. He said, 'Hey, are you a monkey or a chimp?' The animal said, 'I'm a chimp.' And the fellow said, 'I wasn't talking to you!'

A rabbit and a lion went into a restaurant and the rabbit ordered a head of lettuce with no dressing. The waiter said, 'And what will your friend have?' The rabbit said, 'Nothing. He isn't hungry. If he were, do you think I'd be sitting here?'

A man ran over a hare, so he stopped his car, got out and gave the hare a swig from a hip flask. All of a sudden the hare jumped up and ran off into the bushes. His friend said, 'That's amazing! What the hell have you got in that flask?' The man said, 'Hare restorer!'

Antiques

I said, 'You remember that Napoleon bathtub you sold me? Well, I think Napoleon is still in it!' He said, 'Don't be silly. Napoleon's been dead for over a hundred years.' I said, 'Then who's scratching my back?'

Now here's a quick laugh. Do this tomorrow. Walk into an antique shop and shout, 'What's new?'

Army

In the last war I fought and fought ... but I had to go anyway!

If you want to stay out of the army ... join the navy!

I only just avoided a court martial. I was assigned to the officers' party and told to stand at the door and call the officers' names!'

Art

I know he's a sculptor ... I heard someone say, 'There goes that dirty chiseller!'

I did her portrait in oils ...
she has a face like a sardine!

Once I painted a girl in the nude and I almost froze to death!

Anybody can paint oranges ...
I paint the juice!

Asides

Do you think I'm too handsome for my height?

He who laughs last usually has a tooth missing!

After all, what are rich people? Just poor people with money!

I always call a spade a spade, until the other night when I stepped on one in the dark!

Atlantic

This fellow was paddling across the Atlantic in a bathtub when the captain of a liner saw him and yelled out, 'What are you doing?' He said, 'I'm sailing to America.' The captain said, 'You must be crazy. This ocean is very dangerous.' He said, 'I know, but I'm hurrying to catch up with my brother. He's trying to cross in a frying pan!'

Audience Lines

Yes, I know ... I'm crazy – but you paid!

(after applause) Goodness, am I that good? I want more money!

And now for those who came in late ... aren't you glad?

(to a bad audience) I've died in better coffins than this!

Please don't applaud ... it creates a draught!

Any time you want me here again, just say the word ... money!

Well, how do you like that ... a sitting ovation!

You know, these jokes could be worse ... they could be mine!

I'm so confident tonight, I didn't even wear my good suit!

Don't applaud ... I'll lose my place!

I don't care what you think ... I'm staying in show business!

I'd like to say something funny, but I don't want to break the spell!

What a lovely audience ... I'll do the full act tonight! I won't cut a thing!

What an audience! I had them eating out of my hand. They must have thought they were at the zoo!

One night I was doing my act and the whole audience got up and started dancing. And the music wasn't even playing!

After the show we're going to have a competition. You must send in twenty-five words or less on 'Why I like Tommy Cooper.' All entries must be written on a twenty pound note!

Last night I had the audience on their feet ... there was a mouse running up and down the aisle!

I don't have to do this for a living ... but who wants to go back to plucking chickens?

It's not generally known, but one in every four people is a nutcase. So get three friends together and if they're all right ... it's you!

I almost didn't make it here tonight. I had a terrible accident. I fell off the ironing board. I was pressing my trousers and I forgot to take them off!

Now I would like to leave you with an old Norwegian saying, *'Svensky in potorskey ghebin novoja.'* I don't know what it means ... I read it on the back of a tin of sardines once.

(when you stumble over a line) How about that? I had my nose fixed, and now my mouth won't work!

Please be quiet. I've got a sleeping pill in my hand and I don't want to wake it up!

I'm so nervous tonight, I'm afraid I'll say something funny!

If you're in a hurry, don't worry. I've got a pretty fast act ... before you get a chance to hate me, I'll be gone!

I'll never forget the night I made my first appearance as a comedian ... don't think I haven't tried!

Why am I working so fast? I've got the job!

I don't exactly steal jokes ... I just find them before other comedians realise they're missing!

All these jokes are insured against failure, so please laugh or I'll lose my no claims bonus!

That was my best joke ... from here on, it's nerve!

Last night I had an audience! Laugh? I thought they'd never start!

Be patient. My act usually starts slowly ... and then generally peters out!

Audition

A man turned up at an audition and was asked what he could do. He said, 'I do bird impressions.' The producer said, 'Don't waste my time. I don't want any bird imitators on my show.' He said, 'Sorry I bothered you' and flew out of the window.

Australia

A Texan was being shown round this huge farm in Australia. He said, 'This would fit into a small corner of my ranch back in Texas.' Then the Australian showed him his thousands of head of cattle and the Texan said, 'Why, they'd get lost among my herd!' Just then a kangaroo leaped by and the Texan shouted, 'What the hell is that?' The Australian said, 'You mean to tell me you don't have grasshoppers in Texas?'

B is for Balaclava

Bachelor

This bachelor was forty years old and still living at home. His friend said, 'You ought to get yourself a girl.' He said, 'I know, but whatever girl I take home, my mother disapproves.' The friend said, 'Why don't you find a girl just like your mother, then she's bound to like her.' A few months later the bachelor met the friend again and told him he had followed his advice. He said, 'I finally found a girl just like my mother. She looked like my mother, she talked like my mother and she even cooked like my mother.' The friend said, 'So what happened?' He said, 'My father hated her!'

Baker

A guy went into a baker's shop and asked the baker to bake him a cake in the shape of a letter 'K'. The baker told him to come back in a week and the cake would be ready. A week later he went back and saw the cake. He said, 'I'm sorry, but you misunderstood me. I wanted it made in the shape of a small letter "k", not a capital letter "K".' Another week went by and he went back to the shop again. This time he was delighted with the result. The baker said, 'Will you take it with you, sir?' The man said, 'No. Just give me a knife and fork and I'll eat it here!'

Balaclava

Balaclava? I don't know any jokes about a balaclava!

Ballet

My wife wanted to go to the ballet. I said, 'I'm not going to sit and watch a lot of people on their toes in long underwear.' She said, 'You don't have to. Wear your tuxedo.'

All those girls dancing round on their toes ... if they want taller girls, why don't they get them?

My wife said, 'How did you enjoy the ballet?' I said, 'I couldn't hear a word they were saying!'

I've tiptoed into my house so many times at four in the morning, the neighbours think I'm a ballet dancer!

I used to be a ballet dancer. I was priceless in 'Swan Lake' and matchless in Swan Vestas!

Only two things prevented me becoming a dancer myself ... *my feet!*

Banana

Two fellows were on a train. One took out a banana and started to eat it, peel and all. The other said, 'What are you doing? Why don't you peel the banana before you eat it?' The other said, 'Why? I know what's inside.'

Bank

A woman went to the bank to cash a cheque. The cashier said, 'Can you identify yourself?' She took a mirror out of her handbag, looked into it and said, 'Yes, it's me!'

Barbecue

There's a guy having a barbecue in his front garden. He's turning the spit like this and the flames are getting higher and higher – higher and higher – and he's singing, 'Oh sole mio ... O sole mio, farewell.' And the flames are getting higher and higher and this drunk walks by and says, 'Your singing's alright, but your monkey's on fire!'

Barbers

I went into a barber's shop and said, 'How much is a hair cut?' He said, 'Ten pounds.' I said, 'How much is a shave?' He said, 'A fiver.' I said, 'Shave my head!'

A fellow walked into a barber's shop and asked for a shave. This new assistant barber was doing nothing and said, 'How about letting me shave him, boss? It will be good practice.' The boss said, 'Okay, go ahead. But be careful ... don't cut yourself!'

I was telling my barber how I was planning a trip to Italy on one of these economy flights. He said, 'You don't want to do that. The plane will be crowded, the heat is terrible and besides if you think you'll get in to see the Pope, you can forget it.' Three months later I was back in the same barber's. I told him the trip was terrific, the plane was very comfortable and the weather was just right. He said, 'Okay, but did you get in to see the Pope?' I said, 'Yes, and what is more I got a private audience.' He said, 'And what did the Pope say?' I said, 'He said, "Where did you get that lousy haircut?"'

Bathing Beauty

I love bathing beauties, but the trouble is I never bathe any!

Beauty

My wife went to a beauty parlour for a mud pack. It looked so good on her, she wore it for three days!

She has such beautiful unusual lips ... both on top!

She had plastic surgery done on her nose. She had it moved between her eyes!

She had her face lifted so many times, now she talks through her eyes!

She uses pancake make-up ... real pancakes with syrup!

She's always smiling ... she's the only girl I know whose teeth are sunburnt!

She had her face lifted so many times, it's out of focus!

Bequest

This old man was dying and he called his nephew to his bedside. He said, 'I'm leaving you all my money.' The nephew said, 'Thank you, uncle. What can I do for you?' He said, 'Get your foot off my oxygen tube!'

Birds

The early bird catches the worm ... but who wants worms?

Fred Allen used to talk about the bird that flew backwards because it didn't care where it was going ... it was only interested in where it had been. I've got a bird that flies upside down ... if it's shot by a hunter it will fall up instead of down!

Fred Allen knew a farmer who had a scarecrow that scared crows so badly, they brought back corn they had taken two years before!

A man walked into a pet shop and saw a beautiful bird that not only sang beautifully, but also spoke seven different languages. He bought the bird and had it sent home. When he got home later in the day, he said to his wife, 'Did you get the bird I sent home earlier?' She said, 'Yes, I've got it in the oven now.' He said, 'What? In the oven? That bird speaks seven different languages!' She said, 'Well, why didn't he say something?'

Books

I saw a sign in a book shop that read, 'Newly translated from the French ... 27 Mating Positions.' When I got home, it was a book about chess!

I love Shakespeare. I read all his books ... as soon as they come out!

Boxing

I have a photo of myself in the days when I was a boxer. If you turn it sideways it looks as if I'm standing up!

They used to call me Canvasback Cooper. I used to go into the ring vertical and come out horizontal!

They used to call me Rembrandt ... I was always on the canvas!

I did pretty good at the beginning. I won my first ten fights. Then I ran into trouble ... they made me fight a man!

This boxer got a terrible beating in the first round. He staggered to his corner and the manager whispered, 'You won that round.' He got a terrible beating in the second, third and fourth rounds as well and every time the manager said, 'You won that round.' The fifth round was the same ... he was massacred. He staggered back to his corner and the manager said, 'Attaboy, you won that round too.' The boxer said, 'Then tell the referee to give him the next five rounds and call it a draw!'

This fighter sat in his corner between the ninth and last round. His manager said, 'I'm afraid this guy's got you licked.' The fighter looked at his opponent through his half-closed eyes and said, 'Yes, I should have got him in the first round when he was by himself!'

This fighter was knocked to the floor and the referee started the count. When he got to 'Four', his manager shouted, 'Don't get up till "Eight".' He looked up and said, 'Okay, what time is it now?'

My best punch was a rabbit punch, but they wouldn't let me fight rabbits.

I'm in good shape. I can still go ten rounds as long as someone is buying them!

Building

A foreman at a big building site collared one of the workmen and said, 'Hey! How come you're only carrying four bricks at a time, when the others are carrying eight?' He said, 'Well, I guess they're just plain lazy. They're not prepared to make two trips like I do!'

Business

Buddy Hackett has this description of a millionaire friend who got fifty million dollars to sell out his business with the understanding that he wasn't to go into the same business again. So he bought the bank that held the mortgage on the business, then he foreclosed the mortgage and now he's got the business back again!

I just made a terrific deal. I bought up all the heat in town and I'm storing it away till the winter!

C is for Cowboy

Cannibals

They say a cannibal is a guy who loves his fellow man – with gravy!

Did you hear of the cannibal who ate a missionary? He wanted a taste of religion!

The cannibal said, 'My wife made a wonderful pot roast. I'm going to miss her!'

Cars

They've developed a new car ... no clutch, no brakes and no motor. There's only one snag. They can't drive it out of the factory!

When you're driving at night and you see a car coming towards you, dim your headlights. If you can't dim your headlights, turn the radio up real loud!

I got a ticket for parking today ... I haven't even got a car!

I've only had my car three months, but I'll have to buy a new one ... the ashtrays are full!

I bought a car the other day. I said to the guy at the garage, 'All the tyres are flat.' He said, 'Yes, but only at the bottom!'

My wife doesn't really park a car ... she abandons it!

One day my wife came in and said, 'I've got some good news.' I said, 'What's that?' She said, 'You haven't been paying those premiums on the car for nothing!'

Every day she takes the car out, she comes back with the same question ... 'Guess who I ran into?'

One day she said to me, 'I don't want to upset you, but I've got a slight scratch on the bumper.' I asked her to show it to me. She said, 'It's in the boot!'

Last night she backed the car out of the garage perfectly. That would have been okay, but she had just backed it in!

This cop stopped me and said, 'You were doing ninety miles an hour.' I said, 'Don't be silly, officer. This car can't run for an hour!'

Two friends both bought their wives new small cars. When they were delivered, they stood and admired them. One of them lifted the bonnet of her car to see the tiny motor she had heard so much about, but she couldn't see it. She said, 'Mabel, look, they've forgotten to put the motor in my car.' Mabel said, 'Don't worry. I was looking in the boot of my car and I found one there. They must have given me an extra one, so I'll give you one of mine!'

I call my car 'Flattery' ... it gets me nowhere!

Chickens

A man ordered a crate of live chickens. When the farmer delivered them there was no one home, so he left them on the front porch. When the guy came back, the crate was empty and he had to run all over the neighbourhood to catch them. He then rang the farmer. He said, 'Do you know it took me three hours to round them up and I could only find sixteen.' The farmer said, 'What are you complaining about ... I only delivered eight!'

I was walking down the street the other day and I looked over this fence and there was a little chicken, a little Rhode Island Red, and it looked up and went, 'Cluck, cluck.' So I went, 'Cluck, cluck.' And then it went, 'Cluck, cluck' again and I went, 'Cluck, cluck.' Then this policeman came along and arrested us for using foul language!

Childhood

Childhood is that wonderful time when all you have to do to lose weight is to take a bath!

I was a big surprise to my parents. They found me on the doorstep. They were expecting a bottle of milk!

When the nurse told my mother she had an eight pound bundle of joy, she said, 'Thank God, the laundry's back!'

Caerphilly in Wales is the healthiest place in the country. When I first came there I couldn't say a word, I didn't have a single hair on my head and I didn't have the strength to walk across the room. How long was I there? I was born there!

When I was born I was so tough ... when the doctor slapped me, I slapped him back!

When I was a baby I had the cutest little button nose, but they couldn't feed me ... it was buttoned to my lower lip!

I was so shy as a kid, when I was born I was three years old!

I wasn't sure whether my parents disliked me until I came home from school one day and found out they had moved!

I came from a very poor family of five children. We all used to sleep in the same bed. In fact, I never slept alone until I got married.

I never had any luck as a kid. I had a rocking horse once that died!

I had a lead pencil that leaked!

One birthday my father bought me a bat. When I went to play with it, it flew away!

I was different from the kids who were six or seven years old ... I was ten!

I was born with a silver spoon in my mouth ... all the other kids had tongues!

We were so poor my mother used to buy me one shoe at a time.

When I was two I memorised the entire encyclopaedia, but no one believed me because I couldn't talk!

When my father was through explaining about the birds and the bees, he said, 'Are there any questions?' I said, 'Yes ... how can a leopard tell when he's got the measles?'

When I was a kid my father used to give me a penny every day and then he'd pat me on the head. By the time I was fifteen I had twenty quid and a flat head!

My teacher used to tell me that two and two made four. The next day she told me that one and three made four. She never made up her mind!

I came home from school one day and told my father I needed an encyclopaedia. He said, 'Encyclopaedia, my eye! You'll walk to school like everyone else.'

C
D

I used to be afraid of the dark, so my mother always put a lighted candle next to my bed ... now I'm afraid of candles!

I said to my mother, 'Can I go out and play with the child next door?' She said, 'No. You know I don't like the kid next door.' I said, 'Then can I go out and beat the hell out of him?'

One Sunday I came home with my pockets full of cash. My mother said, 'Where did you get that?' I said, 'In church ... they've got plates full of it there!'

My teacher said, 'If there are any idiots in the class, please stand up.' After a while I got up. He said, 'Do you consider yourself an idiot?' I said, 'No ... I just hated to see you standing alone!'

When we were kids we were so tough we used to have pillow fights with bags of nails!

Children

My kids sit and watch television in the living room all day. It's got me worried. Our set is in the bedroom!

The other day my little boy came running up to me shouting, 'Mother has just run over my bicycle while she was backing out of the garage.' I said, 'How many times have I told you not to leave your bike on the front porch?'

The trouble with kids today is they get spoiled too fast. I spent twenty pounds on a space suit for my little boy and then he wouldn't go.

A little boy was standing on a street corner with a cigarette in his mouth and a glass of whiskey in his hand. An old lady came by and said, 'Sonny, why aren't you at school?' He said, 'Because I'm only three!'

A little boy got a watch for his birthday. Someone said, 'That's a pretty watch you've got there ... does it tell you the time?' He said, 'No, this is an old-fashioned watch ... you have to look at it!'

Christmas

I bought my little boy one of those unbreakable toys. It cost me a fortune. He broke every other toy in the house with it!

One Christmas I got a job as Santa Claus in a department store. One little girl sat on my knee and said, 'Guess what I've got.' I said, 'A doll?' She said, 'No.' I said, 'A Christmas list?' She said, 'No.' I said, 'I give up. What have you got?' She said, 'Chickenpox!'

I just finished my Christmas shopping. I bought an electric train set, a scooter, a space helmet and a Meccano set, and I also got some things for the kids.

I said to the girl in the shop, 'I want to give my wife half of a ping pong table for Christmas.' She said, 'Why half a table?' I said, 'She doesn't play!'

Don't forget ... a useful Christmas gift is one that can be exchanged!

It said in the newspaper, 'Do your Christmas shopping early.' So I got up at five o'clock this morning, but all the shops were closed!

All I expect for Christmas is my wife's relations!

And what is the best description of Santa Clause? A blessing in disguise!

Circus

I used to do a juggling act with fifteen clubs, twenty plates and thirty rubber balls. I finally had to give it up. I couldn't figure out what to do with the other hand!

I love the sideshows in the circus. I once saw the tallest man in the world. He was so tall that if he ever fell over he'd have been out of town.

My wife said, 'If you were half a man, you'd take me to the circus ... I said, 'If I were half a man, I'd be in the circus!'

Clothes

This morning I thought the laundry had sent me the wrong shirt. The collar was so tight I could hardly breathe. Then I found out I had my head through a buttonhole!

If you ever saw me in a bathing suit ... I look like a potato with legs!

Boy, you should have seen her dress! I didn't know if she was in that dress trying to get out or outside trying to get in!

My tailor said, 'You're putting on a bit of weight. Why don't you wear a corset?' I said, 'Wear a corset?' He said, 'Yes, that'll pull your stomach in, a corset will.' I said, 'A corset will?' He said, 'O' course it will!'

Do you know why a polar bear wears a fur coat? It would look stupid in tweed!

I surprised my wife with a mink coat. She'd never seen me in one before!

I said to my wife, 'You look just like you looked the day we were married twenty years ago.' She said, 'I should do. It's the same dress!'

I said, 'I know a person who never wears a shirt or a tie but is always well dressed.' She said, 'Who's that?' I said, 'My mother!'

Coffee

I said, 'Waiter, take this coffee away. It tastes like mud.' He said, 'It should do. It was ground only this morning!'

Comedy

Once I took a correspondence course on how to become a comedian. It was supposed to come in ten easy lessons, but I only received the first and the last. I don't know what happened to the other eight, but my postman is playing the Palladium!

Commercials

What I can't work out is how every car, toothpaste and cereal can be better than every other car, toothpaste and cereal?

'Try the new deodorant called "Disappear". After you rub it on once or twice, you will disappear and nobody will know where the smell is coming from!'

'Try our cough mixture ... you'll never get better!'

C
D

Cooking

I miss my wife's cooking ... every chance I get!

She used to go to cookery school, but they threw her out ... she burnt the school!

To cook rice so it won't stick together ... boil it one grain at a time!

I've got a great recipe for pot roast. First brown the roast, then add a fifth of vodka, two quarts of gin, four shots of tequila, a jigger of whiskey, three tablespoons of champagne and then cook for an hour and a half. When it's done ... well, the roast is nothing, but the gravy's delicious!

I won't say she's a lousy cook, but who heard of boiling sardines?

I said to the chef, 'Why have you got your hand in the alphabet soup?' He said, 'I'm groping for words!'

Courtship

When I asked her to whisper those three little words that would make me walk on air, she said, 'Sure ... go hang yourself!'

Her boy friend gave her a big ring ... it holds twenty keys!

Was I surprised when she put her head on my shoulder! I didn't know it came off!

I took her to the pictures and we held hands all through the film. It would have been better if our seats had been together!

I took her to the pictures and it was so exciting, she sat on the edge of her seat all through the movie. She had to. I only bought one ticket!

We had a wonderful candlelight supper. She makes the most delicious candles!

I gave her a bottle of bath salts for her birthday. When I asked her how she liked them, she said, 'Oh, they tasted nice, but I don't think they have the same effect as a real bath!'

Cowboys

You've heard of the Lone Ranger ... I'm his brother, Hydrangea!

I figured out why Zorro rides only at night. He hasn't finished paying for his horse yet!

You know why a cowboy dies with his boots on? So he won't hurt himself when he kicks the bucket!

Crime

The other day I was standing in Piccadilly Circus when I felt a hand in my pocket. I yelled at the guy, 'What's the big idea?' He said, 'I was just looking for a match.' I said, 'Why didn't you ask?' He said, 'Because I don't talk to strangers!'

I knew him well ... we have the same probation officer!

(as Sherlock Holmes:) 'I say, Watson, this is a most serious case ... the window is broken on both sides.'

(as the judge to the beautiful, blonde defendant:) 'Now tell the Jury in your own words how you accidentally happened to stab your husband six times!'

The first cop said, 'Didn't you guard the exits?' The other one said, 'Yes ... he must have got out of one of the entrances.'

A terrorist hijacked a bus full of Japanese tourists and stole all their jewellery. But the police say they should catch him fairly quickly ... they have three thousand photos of him!

A fellow was telling a friend about his three wives and what became of them. He said, 'The first one died of mushrooms, the second one also died of mushrooms, but the third one died from a fractured skull.' He said, 'How was that?' He said, 'She wouldn't eat the mushrooms!'

Three kids were brought before the juvenile court for disturbing the peace. The judge turned to the first one and said, 'What are you here for?' He said, 'Just for throwing peanuts in the water.' The judge said, 'Well, that doesn't seem such a terrible thing,' turned to the second boy and asked him the same question. He said, 'I threw peanuts in the water too.' The judge then turned to the third boy and said, 'And I suppose you threw peanuts in the water also?' He said, 'No, your honour. I am Peanuts!'

I was minding my own business when a fellow came up and poked a gun in my back. He said, 'Stick 'em up!' I said, 'Stick what up?' He said, 'Don't confuse me ... I'm new on the job!'

Customs

A woman was passing through customs. The customs officer said, 'Are you sure, madam, you have nothing to declare?' She said, 'Yes ... absolutely nothing.' He said, 'You mean that the fur tail hanging down from under your dress is your own?'

D is for Dog

Death

Two guys were walking down the street. One said, 'Did you know that Sam died?' The other said, 'No ... did he leave anything?' He said, 'Yes ... everything!'

This old man was sinking fast and as he lay there unconscious, his sons gathered round his bedside to make the arrangements for his funeral. The first one said, 'I can get thirty carriages to the cemetery for a thousand pounds.' The second said, 'We don't need that many carriages. I can get ten for three hundred pounds.' The third son said, 'Now wait a minute, guys. A funeral is only a symbol. We only need five carriages and I can get them for eighty.' The old man opened one eye and said, 'If you'll get me my trousers, I'll get up and walk to the cemetery!'

My aunt died recently and gave me this diamond ring to remember her by. Just look at that sparkle! Just before she died, she said, 'Here's five hundred pounds ... buy the best stone you can find!'

Dentists

I'm always afraid when I go to the dentist. I need an anaesthetic just to sit in the waiting room.

When I asked the dentist to put a cap on my tooth, he put a hat on it!

I always wanted to be a dentist, but my hands were too big. Before I could get to the back teeth I had to pull out all the front teeth.

A woman and her husband went into the dentist's. She said, 'I want a tooth out and I don't want gas because I'm in a dreadful hurry. Just pull the tooth out as quickly as possible so I can be on my way.' The dentist said, 'You're very brave. Which tooth is it?' She turned to her husband and said, 'Get in the chair and show the dentist which tooth.'

He's so healthy, he's got a different dentist for every tooth!

Dieting

There's only one way to diet ... watch your food! Don't eat it. Just watch it!

They've just discovered a new slimming pill. It paralyses your mouth so you can't eat!

When I went on a diet, I ate so much lettuce rabbits were calling me by my first name!

I've lost so much weight, even my shoelaces don't fit!

I'm on a seafood diet ... whenever I see food, I eat it!

I'm on a strict diet ... only one breakfast, lunch and dinner per day!

I'm on a whiskey diet ... last week I lost three days!

I went on an onion diet. I lost ten pounds and twelve friends!

I went on a champagne diet ... in six weeks I lost a thousand pounds!

He lost so much weight, even his toupee looks baggy!

For ten days my wife ate nothing but dog biscuits. She didn't lose any weight, but she's barking much better!

My wife went on a diet of coconuts and bananas. She lost twenty pounds ... just by swinging from chandelier to chandelier!

She's on a diet now. She eats nothing but coconuts and bananas. She hasn't lost any weight, but you should see her climb trees!

I know a guy who took just one slimming pill and lost nine pounds ... his arm fell off!

If you want to lose weight, try skipping ... skipping lunch ... skipping dinner ... !

I know a guy who lost so much weight, even his cufflinks don't fit him any more!

Have you heard about the new four day diet? On the first day you cut out liquids ... on the second day you cut out food ... on the third day you cut out smoking ... and on the fourth day you cut out paper dolls!

I went to a health farm and the first week they gave me nothing to eat. I lost five pounds ... a guy took a bite out of my shoulder!

Divorce

Henny Youngman tells of an eighty-year-old woman who was suing her husband after sixty-two years of marriage. The judge said, 'And you want a divorce now?' She said, 'Yes. Enough is enough!'

I read where a marriage broke up so fast, the bride got custody of the wedding cake!

This woman said, 'Your honour, my husband has beaten me every day for the past year. I'm such a nervous wreck I've lost thirty pounds.' He said, 'And you want a divorce?' She said, 'Yes, but I want to lose another eight pounds first!'

He spent so much time in the doghouse, he finally got his divorce through the RSPCA!

Doctors

I went to see my doctor today. He hasn't been feeling well lately!

My doctor told me to drink a bottle of wine after a hot bath, but I couldn't even finish drinking the hot bath!

I went to the doctor today for a check-up and he said I'm lucky ... if I was a building, I'd be condemned!

A doctor went into the waiting room and found a man with scratches all over his arms, his clothes all torn to shreds and a pelican standing on his head. The doctor said, 'Well, sir, what can I do for you?' The pelican said, 'How can I get this thing off my feet?'

An old man went to the doctor for a check-up and when the doctor finished examining him, he said to the old man, 'You're in good shape. You'll live to be eighty.' The old guy said, 'But I am eighty.' The doctor said, 'See, what did I tell you?'

The doctor said, 'I hope you've been eating lots of fruit with their skins on.' I said, 'Well actually it hasn't been agreeing with me.' He said, 'What have you been eating?' I said, 'Pineapples, coconuts and bananas!'

The doctor said, 'Do you suffer from rheumatism or arthritis?' I said, 'Do you know anybody who enjoys it?'

I said to my doctor the other day, 'One of my legs is shorter than the other. What shall I do?' He said, 'Limp!'

I said, 'Doctor, I keep thinking I'm a monkey wrench.' He said, 'For goodness sake, try and get a grip on yourself!'

I said, 'Doctor, I keep thinking I'm a pair of curtains.' He said, 'Well pull yourself together!'

I said, 'Doctor, I keep thinking I'm a camera.' He said, 'You'll just have to snap out of it!'

I said, 'Doctor, I keep getting these dizzy spells.' He said, 'Vertigo?' I said, 'No, I only live up the road!'

The doctor said, 'How did you hurt yourself?' I said, 'I was up on the roof and I happened to bend down to tie up my shoelaces.' He said, 'How can you hurt yourself that way?' I said, 'My shoes were down on the ground!'

Dogs

I've got a one-man dog ... he only bites me!

I bought a watchdog ... but someone stole the dog!

I sent him to one of those obedience schools and now every time I say, 'Heel,' that's where he bites me!

I've got a dog that can read. The other day it walked past a sign that said 'Wet paint.' He did just what the sign said!

A dog bit a chunk out of my leg the other day. A friend of mine said, 'Did you put anything on it?' I said, 'No, he liked it as it was!'

My dog is harmless really. I say to him, 'Attack!' and he has one!

I've got a very smart dog. All you have to say is, 'Are you coming or not?' and he either comes or he doesn't!

My dog must have belonged to a waiter. He never comes when I call him!

I used to do a dog act. It was so bad the critics used to say that if the dog had any brains he'd do a single.

My uncle was a farmer and he had an old sheep dog. I swear that dog understood every word he said. One day I said to my uncle, 'I swear that dog understands every word you say.' He said, 'Woof, woof!'

I have a sheep dog. Some dogs have fleas ... this one has moths!

Here's to the dog who walked up to a tree
That said to the dog, 'Have one on me!'
But the dog replied, as meek as a mouse,
'No thanks, dear tree. I just had one on the house!'

This fellow took his dog to a theatrical agent and told him the dog could sing and dance and tell jokes. After the audition the agent was so impressed he booked the dog immediately for the London Palladium. While the dog was doing his act, a big dog rushed in, grabbed him and pulled him off the stage. The producer asked the owner what happened and the owner said, 'Oh, that's his mother. She wants him to be a doctor!'

This guy got onto a train and sat opposite an old lady who had a little dog on her lap. It had so much hair, you couldn't tell one end from the other. As soon as he sat down the dog jumped off the lady's lap and bit him on the ankle. The guy didn't say a word. He just put his hand in his pocket and produced a biscuit, which he put on the floor for the dog. The old lady was amazed. She said, 'My word! You are a kind man. My little dog bites you on the ankle and you give him a biscuit.' He said, 'I'm not being kind. I put the biscuit on the floor to find out which end he eats from. Then I can kick the other!'

I bought my wife a lapdog, but she got rid of it. Every time she sat on the dog's lap, it bit her!

I asked the vet why my dog chased cars. He said, 'That's only natural. Most dogs chase cars.' I said, 'I know, but mine catches them and buries them in the garden!'

Do-It-Yourself

My wife is really into Do-It-Yourself. Every time I ask her to fix something, she says, 'Oh, do it yourself!'

My wife does her own decorating, but she overdoes it. The other day I opened the fridge and there was a lamp shade on the light bulb.

Have you heard of those portable home kits? I must have done something wrong. Every time I walked out the front door, I fell off the roof!

Double Gags

I used to juggle plates with one hand.
What did you do with the other hand?
Pick up the pieces!

It's my friend's birthday. I think I'll get him a gold cigarette lighter.
Do you know him that well?
Well, maybe I'll give him a silver lighter.
Is he that good a friend?
I know ... I'll get him a box of matches!

Hey, have you got a new five pound note for an old one?
I sure have.
(makes the exchange and Tommy turns to go)
Just a minute. This is only a one pound note.
I know ... I asked you for a new five pound note for an old one!

Why don't you go to a doctor? They give free operations.
I don't need anything taken out.
Well, have something put in!

I'll never forget the time I fell out of a plane.
That's bad.
Not too bad ... I had a parachute.
That's good.
Not too good ... the parachute didn't open.
That's bad.
Not too bad ... there was a big haystack on the ground below.
That's good.
Not too good ... there was a pitchfork sticking up.
That's bad.
Not too bad ... I missed the pitchfork.
That's good.
Not too good ... I missed the haystack!

My brother used to work in the circus. They used to shoot him out of a cannon.

Was he hurt?

I don't know ... they never found him!

What kind of swimmer are you?

Well, I do the breaststroke for two hours and then I do the crawl for three hours.

And what do you do then?

Then I go in the water and wash the sand off!

You look down. What's bothering you?

I just feel lonely, so lonely that this morning I sat down and wrote myself a letter.

What did you say in it?

I don't know. I won't get it until tomorrow!

I swam the English Channel once.

But a lot of people have swum the Channel.

Lengthwise?

What a night I had! I kept seeing blue snakes and pink elephants.

Have you seen a doctor?

No, only blue snakes and pink elephants!

Take a card. Now I'll write the name of the card you picked on this piece of paper and I'll put it over here. Now think of your card. Got it? Now double it. Okay? Now add your weight. Now double that. Now add your height. Okay? Now divide the number in half. Right? Okay then, what's your card?

The 217 of clubs!

What's the secret of your diet?
Peanut milk!
But how can you get milk from a peanut?
I use a very low stool!

Come down to the river and I'll show you a trick.
What kind of trick?
I'll jump in the water and stay under for three hours.
Three hours under water? You'll drown.
Oh, you know the trick!

Dreams

I had a terrible dream last night. I dreamt my wife and Jayne Mansfield were fighting and my wife was winning!

I had a wonderful dream last night. I dreamt that Brigitte Bardot came up to me and said, 'I will grant you three wishes. Now what are the other two?'

I can't get any sleep ... every time I go to bed I dream I'm awake!

I won't go to sleep for fear I'll dream I'm working!

I dreamt I was eating spaghetti. When I woke up, my pyjama cord had gone!

Last night I dreamt I was a cannon. When I woke up, I shot right out of bed!

Last night I dreamt I was eating a ten pound marshmallow. When I woke up, my pillow had gone!

Once I dreamt I was plucking a chicken. When I woke up, the wife was bald!

Drink and Drunks

C
D

I've been doing some research lately. I drank some whiskey and water and got drunk. Then I drank some brandy and water and got drunk again. Then I drank some rum and water and got drunk a third time. I've come to the conclusion that water must be intoxicating!

A lot of people can't sleep when they drink coffee. With me it's different ... when I sleep, I can't drink coffee!

I almost went blind drinking coffee ... I left the spoon in the cup!

I just had a Boy Scout Cocktail ... two of them and an old lady helps you across the street.

I know a bar where after the fifth drink they give you a test to see if you're sober. They draw a white line on the floor and if you don't trip over it, you're okay!

Two guys were standing at a bar drinking when all of a sudden one of them fell face down on the floor. His friend turned to the bartender and said, 'That's one good thing about him ... he always knows when to stop!'

He can't understand why the Russians don't like us. He takes two vodkas and likes everybody!

He drinks so much, when he blows on a birthday cake he lights the candles!

They say that drinking kills you slowly, but who's in a hurry?

A drunk came out of a nightclub and turned to the porter and yelled, 'Get me a cab.' This big man in uniform said, 'I'm sorry, young man ... I'm not a porter ... I'm an admiral.' The drunk said, 'Well alright then, call me a ship!'

I found a recipe for a hot toddy the other day. It said, 'Take a glass and half fill it with whiskey. Add sugar and lemon to taste, fill the glass with boiling water and place a candle at the foot of the bed. Drink the toddy until you can see three candles. Blow out the middle candle and go to sleep!'

A drunk walked into a bar with a parking meter under his arm. The bartender said, 'You can't bring that in here.' He said, 'I don't want to forget where I parked my car!'

One drunk said to another, 'I don't know what I've done or where I've been, but I wouldn't have missed it for the world!'

This fellow was so drunk he went inside the grandfather clock and tried to make a phone call!

A drunk was brought into a police station. He pounded his fist on the counter and said, 'I want to know why I've been arrested.' The sergeant said, 'You have been brought in for drinking.' He said, 'Oh, that's alright then. Let's get started!'

A drunk was passing a cemetery and saw the sign, 'Ring the bell for the caretaker.' He rang the bell and the caretaker came to the door and said, 'What do you want?' The drunk said, 'I want to know why you can't ring the bell for yourself.'

I'm beginning to realise that drink is a terrible thing. The other day I was in a bar and a big fight started. Chairs and tables were flying through the air. Beer bottles and knives were being thrown all over the place. Everything was being smashed. I would have jumped in and stopped it, but I didn't want to start any trouble!

It's often said that alcohol and petrol don't mix. They do, but it tastes terrible!

How do I look to you? I'm just getting over a severe case of whiskey!

I know my capacity for drinking. The trouble is I get drunk before I reach it!

Why do people call Dean Martin a lush? Just because he has bourbon and cornflakes for breakfast?

I had a very bad accident. I slipped on a piece of ice. I'll never know how I got my foot in the glass!

A guy walked into a bar, ordered a double whiskey, drank it, threw a ten pound note on the table and walked out without saying a word. The barman put the note in his pocket, turned to the owner and said, 'How do you like that? He comes in here, downs a double Scotch, leaves a ten pound tip and then leaves without paying!'

Driving

Watch out for children on the roads ... they're terrible drivers!

I got hit by a hit-and-run driver. The cop said, 'Did you get his number?' I said, 'No, but I'd recognise his laugh anywhere!'

A drunk was driving his car the wrong way down a one-way street when a policeman stopped him. The cop said, 'Didn't you see the arrows?' He said, 'Arrows? I didn't even see the Indians!'

E is for Education

Easter

He said, 'What did you give up for Lent?' I said, 'Fifty pounds for my wife's new Easter bonnet!'

Education

Everybody took an interest in my education. My father wanted me to go to Oxford, my mother wanted me to go to Cambridge and the truant officer wanted me to go to school!

I can't write in the daytime ... I went to night school!

I became a man of letters ... every day I eat alphabet soup!

At the end of the day I asked the teacher, 'What did I learn today?' She said, 'That's an odd question.' I said, 'Yes, but they'll ask me when I get home.'

Whenever the teacher asked a question I was always the first one to raise my hand ... unfortunately, by the time I got back to the room, someone had already answered the question!

My father said to my mother, 'Do you think he gets his intelligence from me?' She said, 'He must do ... I've still got mine!'

I was a genius at school. I had so many original ideas ... especially when it came to spelling!

I always fell asleep when I went to school. My teacher used to say, 'You can't fall asleep in my class.' I said, 'I could, if you didn't talk so loud!'

School days are the happiest days of your life ... provided your kids are old enough to go!

I always had my nose stuck in a book ... I couldn't afford a bookmark!

All I ever wanted out of school was myself!

Elephants

Elephants are remarkable animals. They travel for miles and miles up mountains, through jungles, and across deserts to get to the place where they're going to die and they die there! The trip kills them!

He said, 'How do you make an elephant fly?' I said, 'Well, first find a zip that's three feet long!'

My uncle used to work in the circus. He used to tell me, 'Every morning I'd get up early and carry the elephants to the water.' I said, 'Don't you mean you carried the water to the elephants?' He said, 'No wonder I was tired!'

Two drunks were in a bar. One of them was boasting what a great elephant hunter he was. He said, 'You see, elephants don't like guns. You've got to use psychology and you need four things ... a pair of binoculars, a pair of tweezers, a bucket of water and a bottle of Scotch. Then you find a nice comfortable tree and you put the bucket of water under the tree, climb up onto a big branch and sit there and wait. While you're waiting, you take a drink of Scotch. Pretty soon a big herd of elephants comes along and one elephant always stops to see what's in the bucket at the foot of the tree.' The other drunk said, 'And then what happens?' He said, 'Well, you take another drink of Scotch and then you take the binoculars and turn them around so you're looking through the wrong end. When you see the tiny little elephant at the foot of the tree, you reach down and pick him up with the tweezers. You drop him in the water and he drowns to death!'

E
F

Etiquette

He said, 'Why don't you put your hand over your mouth when you yawn?' I said, 'What ... and get bitten?'

I said, 'Why were you so embarrassed when I dropped that knife in the restaurant? Lots of people drop knives.' He said, 'Not out of their sleeves!'

People ask me what is the difference between politeness and tact. Well, yesterday I walked into the wrong hotel room by mistake. A lady was taking a bath just as I opened the door. I said, 'Excuse me, sir, just like that.' Now, when I said, 'Excuse me,' that was politeness, but when I said, 'Sir,' that was tact!

My wife said, 'When the guests arrive tonight, what should I say – "Dinner is ready" or "Dinner is served"?' I said, 'If you cook like you usually do, "Dinner is ruined!"'

Exercise

I'm in tip-top shape ... but who wants to be shaped like a top?

The doctor said you need a lot of exercise, so I bought myself some golf clubs and my wife a lawnmower!

The doctor asked me what I did to keep fit. I said, 'Every morning I get up at five, I run for five miles, I exercise my arms and shoulders while I'm running, then I come back and go to the gym. I work out for half an hour, then take a cold shower and no matter how hungry I get, I don't eat a thing.' He said, 'How long have you been doing this?' I said, 'I start tomorrow!'

I said to my little boy, 'When I was your age, I thought nothing of walking five miles every day before breakfast.' Well, I don't think much of it now either!

Facts of Life

My little boy asked me how you can tell a boy fish from a girl fish. I said, 'It's all in the worms you use to catch them with. If you bait your hook with a male worm, you catch a female fish and if you use a female worm, you catch a male fish.' He said, 'But how can you tell the difference between a male worm and a female worm?' I said, 'How should I know? I only know about fish!'

When my wife was pregnant we went to see a baby doctor, but he didn't know anything. He was only eight months old!

Every time I start to explain to my little boy about the birds and the bees, he keeps switching the conversation back to girls!

Fairy Stories

A beautiful princess was walking through the woods one day when she came to a pond and heard a tiny frog speak to her. He said, 'Please take me home with you and let me sleep in your bed.' So she picked it up, carried it home and that night she placed it on her pillow. The next morning she had warts!

This fellow had fairies at the bottom of his garden. There were six of them! He used to go down there and count them every night. One night he went down there and he counted, 'One – two – three – four – five ... ' He was a fairy light!

Family

Every morning my mother would get up at seven, eat her breakfast and then go to work. Then my brother Tom would get up, make his breakfast and then he'd go to work. At half past eight my brother Charlie got up, made his breakfast and he'd go to work. Then at nine o'clock my father got up, made his breakfast and he went to work. By that time I had the bed all to myself!

Last week my grandfather celebrated his 103rd birthday. Unfortunately he couldn't be there ... he died when he was thirty-nine!

My grandfather passed away when he was 103. No one expected it. His father was broken up about it!

I hate making decisions. I have an eleven-year-old daughter I haven't named yet!

Family Planning

See Introduction: page 12

Farming

It was so hot on the farm, I milked a cow and got three pints of steam!

Females

She was a gorgeous creature
And he was a doting male.
He admired her figure in English,
But he wanted to prove it in Braille!

Films

You've heard of Hopalong Cassidy ... I want you to meet Dragalong Cooper!

I had a part in 'The Big Sleep' ... I was the mattress!

The movie had a happy ending ... everybody was glad when it was over!

When I was a kid it was much easier to tell right from wrong. The good guys always rode white horses and the bad guys always rode black horses. Then some wise guy came along riding a black and white horse and I've been confused ever since!

Fire

Two businessmen were having a drink. One said, 'I'm sorry to hear about the fire that burned down your factory.' He said, 'Hold your tongue! It's not until tomorrow!'

Fishing

This guy was fishing over a flower bed. I went up and said, 'How many have you caught today?' He said, 'You're the ninth!'

I went fishing the other day and didn't catch a thing. This fellow came up and said, 'Any luck?' I said, 'I could do with a bite!' So he bit me!

Flying

I just flew in ... I should have waited for the plane!

I never go by plane ... I get dizzy just from licking an airmail stamp!

Flying doesn't scare me ... it petrifies me!

I just arrived from America by plane ... it's the only way to fly!

When I complained my ears hurt, the air hostess gave me some chewing gum. I'm still trying to get it out of my ears!

I was relaxing in the plane watching the clouds go by when a parachutist appeared in the aisle. He said, 'Are you going to join me?' I said, 'Thank you very much, but I'm happy where I am.' The parachutist said, 'Just as you like ... I'm the pilot!'

I always sit in the back of a plane. It's much safer. You never hear of a plane backing into a mountain!

Food

Did you ever try to eat with chopsticks? I tried it once. I didn't eat anything, but I started three fires!

The most important thing in life is food. If you ever stop to think about it, without food you can't eat!

Fortune Tellers

She told me she reads tea leaves. I didn't even know you could write on them!

I went to a fortune teller and she looked at my hands. She said, 'Your future looks pretty black!' I said, 'Are you kidding? I've still got my gloves on!'

Friends

He's the kind of friend you can always depend on ... always around when he needs you!

G is for Giraffe

Gambling

In Las Vegas they gamble everywhere. I went into a drug store for an aspirin and the girl behind the counter said, 'I'll toss you, double or nothing.' I lost. I came out with two headaches!

When I was in Las Vegas I was so unlucky I even lost money in the stamp machine!

Gambling has brought our family closer together. We had to move to a smaller house!

He's a second-hand dealer. The first hand he lets you win. But watch out for that second hand!

This fellow went into a betting shop and put one hundred pounds on a horse at twenty to one ... and he won two thousand pounds. He collected his winnings, came out of the shop and bumped into an old tramp. He said, 'Oh, I'm sorry. I've just won two thousand pounds on a horse and I was so excited I didn't see you.' The tramp said, 'Two thousand pounds?' He said, 'Yes, would you like to hold it for a moment?' The tramp said, 'I'd love to ... just to feel it in my hands for a moment ... two thousand pounds!' As he moved forward to take the money, the tramp suddenly turned white and fainted. A woman passed by and said, 'What's wrong with him?' The guy said, 'I don't know. He didn't feel two grand!'

Gardening

I took up gardening and all I grew was tired!

I love the sound of a lawnmower. It means that something is being done and I'm not doing it!

One day I was spraying my lawn and my neighbour asked me what I was using. I said, 'It's a secret formula to keep away elephants.' He said, 'But we don't get elephants around here.' I said, 'See how effective it is!'

There's nothing I like more on a warm summer's day than to put on my old clothes and a big shady hat, get out all the tools, settle down in a deckchair with a long cool drink and then tell the gardener where to dig!

Ghosts

These two ghosts used to walk around together with their heads under their arms. One day they slept late, got up in a hurry and grabbed the wrong heads. Later that night, one of them said, 'Here, guess what I've done?' The other said, 'I already know. I'm ahead of you!'

Giraffe

Do you know what's worse than a giraffe with a sore throat? A centipede with fallen arches!

Girls

I took her to Paris to see the Venus de Milo. She said, 'I'd like to look like her.' So I broke both her arms!

She's a cover girl ... the more her face is covered, the better she looks!

Golf

I played a little golf this morning. First I teed off and I made a hole in one. Then I teed off again and I made another hole. Then I covered up both holes and went home!

The other day I got caught in a bunker and couldn't get out. The more I tried to hit the ball, the deeper I got into the bunker. The caddy said, 'What are you doing? Digging for **diamonds**?' I said, 'Have a **heart**!' He said, 'Do you want a **club**?' I said, 'No, a **spade**!'

When I first took up golf I dug up so many worms I decided to go fishing!

I once had a caddy who kept laughing at all my strokes. I would have knocked his head off, but I didn't know which club to use!

I saw a sign on a Scottish golf course once. It said, 'Members will please refrain from picking up lost balls until after they have stopped rolling!'

I said to the caddy, 'Do you think I can get home with a 4 iron?' He said, 'I don't know ... where do you live?'

The Scotsman said to the caddy, 'How are you at finding lost balls?' He said, 'Very good, sir!' The Scotsman said, 'Well, look around and find one and we'll start the game!'

When you're swinging a golf club, there are three rules always to remember – one, keep your head down; two, keep your damn head down; and three, keep your goddamn head down.

I found out why you have to address the ball ... so that if you lose it, they'll mail it to you!

As Jack Benny once said, give me my golf clubs, the fresh air and a beautiful partner and you can keep my golf clubs and the fresh air!

I went into a shop and bought a golf ball. The man said, 'Shall I wrap it?' I said, 'No, I'll drive it home!'

H is for Hats

Hair

Being bald has its advantages ... you're the first one to know when it starts raining!

I used to part my hair from ear to ear. It was okay, but people kept whispering in my nose!

Halloween

On Halloween I really know how to scare people. I ring their bell and do my act!

Hats

Somebody gave me a ten gallon hat. I didn't know whether to wear it or move into it!

My wife said, 'Do you like this turned down hat?' I said, 'How much does it cost?' She said, 'Fifty pounds.' I said, 'Turn it down!'

There's nothing that goes to my wife's head faster than a new hat!

She said, 'Your hat is on the wrong way.' I said, 'How do you know which way I'm going?'

I said to the girl in the shop, 'I want to buy a hat.' She said, 'Fedora?' I said, 'No, for myself!'

She wore a hat with so many flowers on it, three funerals followed her home!

They're making a new kind of woman's hat with a live pigeon on top. If you don't pay the bill, the hat flies back to the shop!

Health

He suffers from an occupational disease. Work makes him sick!

I'm recovering from a cold. I'm so full of penicillin that if I sneeze, I'll cure someone.

Every morning I like a cold bath ... filled with hot water!

I found a good cure for amnesia, but I can't remember what it is!

The best way to avoid a cold is to drink a lot of water. You never saw a fish with a cold!

All his life he had trouble with his back ... he couldn't get it off the bed!

I'm so anaemic. The other day a guy hit me on the nose. I said, 'I owe you a nose bleed!'

Heaven

This fellow died and went to heaven. When he got there, St Peter told him that before he'd be allowed in, he'd have to take a test. First, he'd have to fly twenty yards with the wings they gave him, then play three choruses of his favourite hymn on a harp, and finally walk a hundred paces with a halo on his head without it slipping. Well, he passed the flying without any trouble and played not three, but six choruses of the hymn on the harp, but he just couldn't get the halo to stay straight when he walked. St Peter said, 'I'm sorry, we can't accept you.' The fellow said, 'Why?' St Peter said, 'Well, you're very good, but before you come in you have to get your "O" level!'

Heckler-Squelchers

Some people might think you're loud and foolish ... and I agree with them!

There's a rumour going around that he had a mother!

He's good to his mother ... he brings home everything he steals!

Did you ever get the feeling that the world was a tuxedo and you were a pair of brown shoes?

I live down by the river. If you're in the neighbourhood, drop in!

(to a drunk) It's great to see a guy who can hold his lemonade like a man!

I'd put you in your place, if only I had the time and a shovel!

Was the ground cold when you came out of it this morning?

It's lucky for you I'm a gentleman ... and a coward!

Hobbies

I've got a special hobby. You know how some people collect stamps and some people collect paintings? Well, I collect dust!

Hollywood

Fred Allen once said, 'You could take all the sincerity in Hollywood and conceal it in a flea's navel and still have enough room left for six caraway seeds and an agent's heart.'

Home

I live in one of those reversible penthouses. It's in the basement!

My agent ... his home is so big, when it's five o'clock in the kitchen, it's six o'clock in the living room!

Honesty

Honesty is the best policy. The only time I ever found anything ... it was a wallet with a hundred pounds. So I put an ad in the 'lost and found' column of a newspaper ... the Budapest Times!

I wouldn't believe him if he swore he was lying!

Horses

You know what a racehorse is ... an animal that can take several thousand people for a ride at the same time!

I bought a racehorse about a month ago. A friend of mine said, 'What are you going to do with it?' I said, 'I'm going to race it.' He said, 'By the look of it, I think you'll beat it!'

This fellow bet two thousand pounds on a horse and lost. I said, 'How do you feel?' He said, 'Not too grand!'

I used to have a riding school, but business kept falling off!

She said, 'Your wife won't talk to me since I took her horseback riding.' I said, 'She could be sore about something.'

I was born in the saddle ... and it wasn't easy!

I bet on a horse that was so slow. The jockey kept hitting it with his whip and the horse said, 'What are you doing that for? There's nobody behind us!'

A man paid £5,000 for a racehorse and entered it in a £10,000 race. The horse came last. So he entered it in a £5,000 race and it came last again. So he entered it in a £1,000 race and it came last once more. He went to the horse and said, 'Look, I'm going to enter you in a £500 race and if you lose this one, tomorrow morning you'll be pulling a milk cart.' The race began and the horse was so far behind that the jockey began to hit him with the whip. The horse looked back and said, 'Hey, take it easy ... I've got to be up at five o'clock!'

Hospitals

I saw a sign in a hospital the other day that read, 'Visitors only from two to five.' Isn't that silly? Who wants visitors that young?

Hotels

I've stayed at every hotel in the country and I've got the towels to prove it!

The hotel was fine, but the towels were so thick, you couldn't close your suitcase!

I stayed at a hotel and they gave me a room facing north ... it had no roof!

I couldn't sleep ... too many people kept coming in all night to wash their hands!

I said, 'Is this room service?' The girl said, 'Yes.' I said, 'Send up a room.'

There was a sign in the room: 'Don't slam the door ... it's holding up the walls!'

It was really warm in my room. I tried to open the window, but it was stuck. It wouldn't budge. So I finally took an aspirin to ease the pane!

I said to the porter, 'What's the idea of giving me one black shoe and one brown shoe?' He said, 'I'm sorry, sir. That's the second time that's happened this morning!'

I said to the receptionist, 'Is the room rate really ten pounds a day?' She said, 'No, it's ten pounds for the night ... we throw the day in for free.'

I went into my room and rang straightaway for the manager. I said, 'Does the water always come through the roof like that?' He said, 'Only when it rains!'

This hotel was so big, by the time I got to my room I owed two days rent!

I said to the receptionist, 'I want a full-length mirror put in my room right away.' She said, 'But you've already got a half-length mirror. What's wrong with that?' I said, 'Three times this week I've gone out without my trousers on!'

My room was so small I couldn't brush my teeth sideways!

Hypochondria

A hypochondriac went to see his doctor. The doctor said, 'Well, what do you think is the matter with you today?' He said, 'I don't know ... what's new?'

I knew a hypochondriac who wouldn't visit the Dead Sea until he found out what it died of!

He's such a hypochondriac, he has a vaccination before he goes to a foreign movie!

I is for Indian

Ignition

Two drunks were sitting at a bar when one said to the other, 'Does your tongue burn?' The other said, 'I don't know. I've never been drunk enough to light it!'

Indians

The Lone Ranger and Tonto rode into a spot of bother. On all sides they were surrounded by hostile Indians. The Lone Ranger said, 'Well, kemosabe, it looks like the end of the trail. Those Indians are about to close in. We've had it.' Tonto said, 'You mean you've had it, white man!'

An Indian chief walked into a restaurant. The waiter said, 'Do you have a reservation?' He said, 'Certainly ... in Arizona!'

There was an Indian chief called Running Water. He had two sons named Hot and Cold and a nephew, Lukewarm!

An Indian chief had two sons, Straight Arrow and Falling Rocks. The day came when he told them to go out into the world and make a name for themselves. In time Straight Arrow came back, but Falling Rocks never returned. They're still looking for him. That's why everywhere you go in the Wild West you see signs saying, 'Watch out for Falling Rocks'!

Insects

I feel like a mosquito in a nudist colony ... I don't know where to begin!

Two fleas were going shopping. One said, 'Shall we walk or take a dog?'

Insomnia

My insomnia is getting
so bad, I can't even
sleep when it's time
to get up!

I'm cured now, but
I lie awake half the
night thinking of
how I used to suffer
from it!

If you've got insomnia,
don't lose any sleep
over it!

They've got a new
cure for insomnia ...
a pill that weighs two
hundred pounds.
You don't swallow it.
You drop it on your
head!

I couldn't sleep a
wink last night.
I took a sleeping pill
and I dreamt all night
that I was awake!

I was awake half the night trying to remember something I wanted to do. Then about five o'clock in the morning it suddenly dawned on me ... I had planned to go to bed early!

Insults

As for my agent, I've seen poultry better dressed than he is!

He's so tightfisted, he's got varicose veins in his knuckles!

Insurance

I

J

I've got the only policy that pays me a thousand pounds if I get hit by a satellite while singing 'How High the Moon'!

I'm covered with insurance policies up to here. One day I'll cover the rest of me!

I cancelled my Fire Insurance Policy because they wouldn't pay a claim. I claimed that all the cigars I smoked last year were destroyed by fire!

Burglars broke into our house and I was told I couldn't collect a penny. The agent said I had Fire and Theft policies, when I should have had Fire or Theft. That means the only way I'd collect would be if we were robbed while the house was burning down!

Insurance policies are great. You pay and you pay and when you die you have nothing to worry about for the rest of your life!

An insurance salesman wants to sell me a retirement policy. If I keep up the payments for ten years, he'll be able to retire!

I said, 'I've just taken out a £10,000 policy.' He said, 'Accident?'
I said, 'No – on purpose!'

I have a policy that states that if I bang my head, they pay me a lump sum!

Interior Decorator

This woman went to an interior decorator and had great trouble getting
what she wanted. She finally opened up and confessed that her husband
thought he was a bear. The decorator said, 'A bear? Why don't you go to
a psychiatrist?' She said, 'Do you think he can tell me what colour
scheme will work in a cave?'

Introductions

She plays the piano by ear ... but sometimes her earrings get in the way!

Our next act needs no introduction, because he hasn't shown up!

Our next act comes to us direct from America where he was hailed by
thousands of people. He was driving a taxi!

Five producers wanted our next act to go to Hollywood and make a picture,
but they found out she couldn't paint!

After playing the accordion all his life, our next act took up the piano.
Every time he hung it round his neck, it nearly killed him!

It gives me great pleasure to introduce our next act. We will now have
a one minute intermission to give you all a chance to say, 'Who cares?'

He has been in films, he has been on radio, he has been on television ... he's probably the biggest has-been in the business!

There's no end to his talent ... and no beginning either!

Inventions

I've just invented a chemical that is so powerful it destroys anything it touches ... but I can't find anything to keep it in!

I've just invented a new noiseless alarm clock. It doesn't ring. It has a big eye that stares at you till you wake up!

I've just invented a pen with a meatball point. It writes under gravy!

I've just invented a stepladder without steps for cleaning windows on the ground floor!

My father invented a burglar alarm, but someone stole it!

The thermos flask is a great invention. How does it know when to keep things hot and when to keep them cold?

Electricity is a wonderful thing. Do you realise that if we didn't have electricity, we'd be watching television by candlelight?

I see they've invented a new cigarette. The whole thing is a filter ... only the tip contains tobacco!

I've just invented plastic song sheets ... for people who like to sing in the shower!

J is for Jester

Jester

What do you call an out-of-work jester? Nobody's fool!

Jewellery

A shoplifter was caught stealing a watch. He begged the jeweller not to call the police and said he would happily pay for it. He was taken to the cashier and given a bill. He took one look and said, 'Goodness, that's a little more than I can afford. Can't you show me something a little cheaper?'

Jobs

I said to my boss, 'My wife and I find it very hard for two people to live on my salary.' He got us a divorce!

The boss asked me how much I wanted, so I quoted him a price in six figures. He picked one and we made a deal!

He used to be a night-watchman, but he got fired. Someone stole two nights!

He says he has hundreds of people under him ... he's a watchman in a cemetery!

It must be wonderful to be an undertaker. Where else can you go to work and find everything laid out for you?

There was this fellow. One day his wife said, 'Get out of bed and get a job.' His friend said, 'So what happened? Did you go out and get a job?' He said, 'Are you kidding? Where can you find a job at five o'clock in the afternoon?'

This chap was out of work. He couldn't get a job anywhere. Then one day he was walking along the road and he passed this building site. He went up to this fellow who was working there and said, 'Excuse me, I was wondering if you were looking for any men for this job.' The fellow said, 'Well, as it happens, they are looking for labourers. Why don't you see the foreman over there? He'll fix you up. But there's just one thing. It's a company rule. They'll only take you on if you know someone who's already working on the site. Otherwise you're wasting your time.' So he walked across to the foreman and said, 'Excuse me. I was wondering if there were any jobs going.' The foreman said, 'As a matter of fact there are. When can you start?' He said, 'Straightaway.' The foreman said, 'Right! By the way there's just one thing. We only take on people who know someone already working on the site. Is there anyone here you recognise?' The chap didn't know a soul, but he suddenly heard this Irish guy working nearby. He said, 'I know him!' The foreman said, 'What's his name then?' He said, 'His name is Dare.' The foreman said, 'Well, give him a call.' The chap said, 'Alright.' So he gave the Irishman a wave and shouted, 'Hallo, Dare.' The Irishman replied, 'Hallo dare yourself!' and the chap got the job!

I know a guy who has the hardest job in the world. He sells Venetian blinds for submarines.

I got a job once selling doorbells door to door. Unfortunately when I rang, the people who needed what I had to sell didn't know I was there!

Jokes on Jokes

You know what you have to go through to be a comedian? A lot of old joke books!

My wife knows my jokes backwards ... and that's how she tells them!

Jungley!!

A big lion was roaring through the jungle one day with this chip on his shoulder. Every animal he came across, he'd stop them and say, 'Who is the King of the Jungle?' and he was told that he was. Finally he bumped into a mean, nasty-tempered elephant. So he stopped him and said, 'Hey, Jumbo, who is the King of the Jungle?' So the elephant grabbed the lion with his trunk, tossed him into the air half a dozen times and then slammed him against a big tree. The lion picked himself up and said, 'Look, there's no good getting sore about it, just because you don't know the answer!'

I
J

A hunter came across a lion in the jungle and began to pray. Then the lion started to pray too. He turned to the hunter and said, 'Don't get me wrong ... I always say grace before meals!'

Two guys – Tom and Harry – went lion hunting in Africa and one night Harry bet Tom a fiver that he'd be the first one to go out and kill a lion. They made the bet and Harry went out with his rifle. After about an hour, a lion poked his head into the tent and said, 'Hey, do you know a guy named Harry?' Tom said, 'Yes, I do. Why?' and the lion said, 'Well, he owes you a fiver!'

Two guys were hunting for lions in Africa and got themselves a hut right on the edge of the jungle. After a short while one of them was seen tearing back to the hut with a big roaring lion running after him. The hunter fell through the open door and the lion shot past him into the hut. Quick as a flash, the hunter got up, rushed outside and slammed the door behind him. As he ran off, he yelled back to his friend inside, 'You skin that one, while I go after another one!'

K is for Karate

Kangaroos

He said, 'What does a kangaroo eat for breakfast?' I said, 'I don't know.' He said, 'Pouched eggs!'

A mother kangaroo turned to her friend and said, 'I hate it when it's raining and the kids have to play inside!'

A kangaroo kept escaping from his enclosure at the zoo. The keepers put up this fence that was ten feet high, but the kangaroo still escaped. The next day they put up a twenty-foot fence, and he still got free. The monkey in the next enclosure said, 'How high do you think they'll go?' The kangaroo said, 'It doesn't matter until someone remembers to lock the gate at night!'

He said, 'Why was the mother kangaroo cross with her children?' I said, 'I don't know.' He said, 'Because they ate biscuits in bed!'

Karate

I always say that if you practise breaking boards in half with your bare hand, you'll be able to look after yourself when a board attacks you!

I know a priest who took up karate. He became so good at it, when he went to bless himself he broke his nose!

My wife is so good at karate, last week she stuck her hand out to make a left turn and cut a truck in half!

Then there was the karate expert who joined the army. When he gave his first salute, he killed himself!

When I first met my wife, I got a lump in my throat ... she was a karate expert!

Kissing

She said, 'How come when I kiss you your lips burn like fire?' I said, 'Well, maybe I ought to take the cigarette out of my mouth!'

I asked her how she learned to kiss like that. She said she used to blow up footballs!

She said, 'Who told you that you could kiss me?' I said, 'Just about everybody!'

Kleptomania

A kleptomaniac was treated by a psychiatrist and after a while he was discharged as cured. He said, 'I'd like to do something for you to show my gratitude.' The doctor said, 'Well, I really don't want anything, but if you ever get a relapse, I could use a transistor radio!'

Knight

In days of old when knights were bold ... the king turned to his knight and said, 'What have you been doing today?' The knight said, 'I have been robbing and pillaging on your behalf, burning the villages of your enemies in the north.' The king said, 'But I don't have any enemies in the north.' The knight said, 'I'm afraid you do now!'

Knowledge

Did you know that a female herring lays about 35,000 eggs at one time? If those herrings were a little bit smarter, they could take over the world!

People learn something new every day ... why just today my wife learned that a car won't climb a telephone pole!

I'm studying anthropology. I went into our local library and said, 'Do you keep books on pygmies?' The girl said, 'No, only on shelves!'

Space is where there is nothing. I can't exactly explain it to you, but I've got it right here in my head!

L is for Law

Languages

I learned Japanese with records that play while you sleep. It works. Now I speak perfect Japanese, but only when I'm asleep!

This rich old lady sent her pet poodle to a language school to learn a foreign language. Her friend said, 'This is ridiculous. How can a poor dumb animal learn a foreign language?' and the poodle looked up and said, 'Meow!'

Laundry

I feel like a changed man ... I just got my laundry back!

I was really surprised when my laundry sent back a dozen shirts without a single button missing. I only sent them a pair of shorts!

I always get my laundry back the same day. They keep refusing it!

Jack the Ripper never died ... he's doing my shirts!

Law

A man was brought into court for disturbing the peace. The judge said, 'What I would like to know is what induced you to climb to the top of a flagpole, play the saxophone, shout at the people walking by and disturb everyone by singing at the top of your voice.' He said, 'Well, it's like this, your honour. If I didn't do something like this once in a while, I'd go crazy!'

The judge asked the defendant why he hit his wife with a heavy lamp. He said, 'Because the piano was too heavy!'

The jury returned to the courtroom after being out for three days. The judge said, 'Have you reached a decision?' The foreman said, 'Yes, your honour. We've decided not to become involved.'

He said, 'I'm a lawyer of twenty years standing.' I said, 'You must be tired ... sit down!'

The lawyer asked the prisoner what his trade was. He said, 'I'm a locksmith.' Then the lawyer asked him what he was doing inside the premises when the police raided them. He said, 'I was making a bolt for the door!'

The first lawyer said, 'As soon as I realised it was a crooked business, I got out of it.' The second lawyer said, 'How much?'

The judge said to the pickpocket, 'How is it you took that man's watch from his pocket without him knowing it?' He said, 'I can't give out that information, your honour. My fee is one hundred pounds for the full course of ten lessons!'

Laziness

I'm not afraid of hard work. I could fall asleep right beside it!

This guy said, 'Are you in favour of a five day week?' I said, 'No. I'm in favour of a five day weekend!'

The fellow next door said, 'What was that terrible noise I heard at your house last night?' I said, 'That was my wife washing my clothes.' He said, 'Why should that cause so much noise?' I said, 'I was too lazy to get out of them!'

I missed my nap today. I slept right through it!

Letters

Dear Agony Aunt, Ten years ago I sent my husband out for a loaf of bread and he hasn't come back since. What shall I do? ... *Don't wait any longer. Send out for another loaf of bread!*

Liar

This guy said, 'If a fellow called you a liar, what would you do?' I said, 'What size fellow?'

Library

K
L

Society people usually have dinner at eight and then coffee is served in the library. I always thought the library closed at seven!

I said to the librarian, 'Have you got a book on butterflies?' She said, 'Yes.' I said, 'Well, take it off ... you'll crush them to death!'

Love Bites

See Introduction: page 12

Luck

I'm so unlucky ... one day I called the speaking clock and the recording hung up on me!

I'm the sort of fellow who gets paper-cuts from get well cards!

GET ME TO THE CHURCH ON TIME!

M is for Marriage

Marriage

They've been married for twenty years and they still feel the same – they can't stand each other!

This woman was dying. She called her husband to her bed and said, 'Sam, I've been unfaithful to you.' He said, 'So? What do you think I gave you poison for?'

There were ten chorus girls. Nine of them married millionaires. They got diamonds, furs, expensive holidays. Only one of them married a poor man. And, would you believe it, she's the only one who's miserable!

This guy bought his wife a burial plot for her birthday. The following year when he bought her nothing, she complained. He said, 'What are you complaining about? You didn't use the present I bought you last year!'

This woman went on holiday leaving her husband behind. Before she left she told him to take special care of her pet Siamese cat. As soon as she arrived she phoned home to ask after the cat. Her husband said, 'The cat just died!' She burst into tears and started to read the riot act to him: 'How can you be so blunt? Why couldn't you have broken the news gradually? Today you could have said it was playing on the roof. Tomorrow you could have added that it fell off the roof and broke a leg. Then on the third day you could have said the poor thing had passed away in the night. You could have been more sensitive about the whole thing. By the way, how's my mother?' He said, 'She's playing on the roof!'

We've been married for 20 years and she still wears a ponytail. She's certainly got the face for it!

Memory

My memory's terrible. I have to look at the mail before I can remember my own name!

Every comedian comes out and says, 'A funny thing happened to me on the way to the theatre this evening.' Well, a funny thing happened to me on the way to the theatre this evening ... I forgot my act!

My wife has a terrible memory. She never forgets a single thing she tells me to do!

I've got a terrible memory. I cut myself shaving today and I forgot to bleed!

Men

He never smiles. Not because he has bad teeth ... it's just that his gums don't fit!

He has a speech impediment ... every time he opens his mouth his wife interrupts!

He may talk like an idiot and look like an idiot, but don't let it fool you ... he is an idiot!

I know a guy who shaves thirty times a day ... he's a barber!

Money

I know a guy whose wife made him a millionaire ... before that he was a multi-millionaire!

I made a killing in the stock market ... I shot my broker!

The mechanic gave me an estimate of one hundred pounds to fix my car. The next day he gave me a bill for two hundred. I said, 'How about the estimate you gave me yesterday for one hundred?' He said, 'Oh yes, I forgot! That makes it three hundred!'

Money isn't everything. I've got something money can't buy ... poverty!

Motorcycle

The trouble with my wife is that she's a terrible backseat driver ... so I decided to buy a motorbike and sidecar. But this didn't stop her going yackety-yak all the time. Yackety-yak! Yackety-yak! One day a policeman pulled me over and said, 'Hey, your wife fell out of the sidecar six miles back.' I said, 'Thank God! I thought I was going deaf!'

Music and Musicians

He's one of the best arrangers in the business. He arranges all the chairs for the band!

He used to have a three piece combo ... an organ, a cup and a monkey!

I asked the pianist if he played by ear. He said, 'No, my neck isn't long enough!'

Now I'm going to play like I've never played before ... because I've never played before!

For years I used to run up and down the scales with my fingers. I used to work in a fish shop!

M
N

I used to be a one man band. I played the drums with my feet, the harmonica with my mouth, the tambourine with my elbows and the vibraphone with my knees. *What did I do with my hands?* I held them to my ears!

Some people can make a piano talk, but I can make a piano laugh ... I tickle the ivories!

I can tell the time from my piano. Every morning when I start to play someone bangs on the wall and yells, 'Hey, stop making that noise at two o'clock in the morning!'

I bought a piano stool the other day ... I can't get a single note out of it!

When I play the accordion I always cry ... it keeps pinching my stomach!

He plays the hottest trumpet in town ... he stole it only last week!

My uncle was a great conductor ... he was struck by lightning!

He's a relief piano player ... it's a relief when he stops!

When I was in New York, a fellow walked up to me and said, 'Excuse me, but how do you get to Carnegie Hall?' I said, 'Practice!'

I took saxophone lessons for six months until I dislocated my jaw. How did I know I was supposed to blow in the small end?

A piano tuner was called to a nightclub to tune the piano. He was at it for five hours, but the bill only came to three pounds. The manager said 'Is that all? How come you worked for five hours to tune the piano and you only charge three pounds?' He said, 'What?'

N is for Night

Neighbours

The only time we see our neighbours is when we try to borrow back our lawnmower!

Night

A hunter woke up a farmer in the middle of the night and yelled, 'I'm sorry to wake you, but it's very cold and I'd like to stay here for the night.' The farmer slammed down the window and said, 'Well, stay there!'

Nudist

This fellow went up to a nudist colony and said, 'I want to join.' The guy on the gate said, 'You can't join with that blue suit on.' He said, 'What blue suit? I'm cold!'

Numbers

Seven's my lucky number. I was born on the 7th day of the 7th month in the year 1917. Last night I dreamed I kissed 7 girls, so today I bet on the 7th horse in the 7th race. The horse was called 'Seventh Heaven.' It came in seventh!

I'm a member of the Secret Six. It's so secret, I don't even know the other five!

Nurse

When I had a cold I rang the doctor and the nurse answered. I said, 'I think I have a temperature.' She said, 'Take off all your clothes and get into bed!' *But she never showed up!*

Nursery Rhymes

There was an old woman
Who lived in a shoe,
She had so many children
Her baby sitters' bill came to goodness knows how many pounds!

Little Miss Muffet
Sat on a tuffet,
Eating her curds and whey;
Along came a spider,
Who sat down beside her ...
... 'Is this seat taken?'

Little Miss Muffet
Sat on a tuffet,
Around her was fog and mist;
Along came a spider,
Who sat down beside her
And offered to teach her the Twist!

Mary had a little lamb ...
... boy, was she surprised ... she was expecting a baby!

Mary, Mary, quite contrary,
How does your garden grow?
... 'None of your damn business!'

Little Jack Horner
Sat in a corner
Eating his Christmas pie.
He put in his thumb
And pulled out a plum
And said, 'But I ordered apple!'

Jack was nimble,
Jack was quick,
Jack jumped out of the window quick ...
... her husband came home!

Thirty days have September,
April, June and November.
All the rest have thirty-one
...except Jane Russell, who has a perfect 36!

Rock-a-bye, baby,
On the tree top,
When the bough breaks ...
... you'll shout 'Timber!' if you've got any sense!

Roses are red,
Violets are blue,
Orchids cost three-fifty,
Won't daisies do?

Jack and Jill
Went up the hill.
The last I heard
They were up there still!

Old King Cole was a merry old soul
And a merry old soul was he.
He called for his pipe
And he called for his bowl
And he called and he called and he called ... !

Humpty Dumpty sat on a wall,
Humpty Dumpty had a great fall;
All the King's horses
And all the King's men ...
... had scrambled eggs!

O is for One - Liner

One-Liners

I said, 'Don't you recognise me?' He said, 'Is there a reward?'

I've got news for you ... I just heard from Bill Bailey and he isn't coming home!

I feel like doing something wild tonight ... like taking a bath in Pepsi Cola!

He's a second-hand dealer. The first hand he lets you win, but watch out for that second hand!

I went into a country pub yesterday and ate a ploughman's lunch. He wasn't half mad!

I'm tired ... I've been on my feet all day. It's the only way I can stand up!

I'm not myself tonight ... you probably noticed the improvement!

I'm tired – I got up the wrong side of the floor!

Where there's smoke – there's toast!

I'm so excited about my new job, I won't be able to sleep all day!

Time is relative. I know – I've got a relative doing time!

I served 87 cups of tea – I must get a new tea bag!

He offered me a job right up my alley, but who wants to work up an alley?

It was so foggy in Scotland, this fellow milked three cows before he found out he wasn't playing the bagpipes!

Onions

Do you know the
difference between a
lawyer and an onion?
You cry when you cut up
an onion!

My wife is so ugly she
made an onion cry!

Opera

This singer went to
Rome to study opera. When he sang his first aria in pub-
lic, the audience shouted, 'Sing it again,' so he obliged. Again they yelled,
'Sing it again,' so he sang it a second time. This went on for half a dozen
times until he begged to be excused. He said, 'I'm sorry, I just can't sing
it again!' Then a voice in the balcony yelled out, 'You're going to sing it
again until you get it right!'

I took my little boy to the opera. The conductor started to wave his baton
and the big fat lady on the stage started to sing her heart out. He said,
'Dad, why is he hitting that woman with that stick?' I said, 'He isn't
hitting her. He's just conducting the band.' My little boy said, 'Then what
is she screaming for?'

The other night I went to the opera ... that's where, when a guy gets
stabbed, he doesn't bleed, he sings!

I was in an opera once. I was in *The Barber of Seville*. I played a jar of
Brylcreem!

Operating Theatre

A medical student was working his way through college by moonlighting in a butcher's shop. He worked in the butcher's shop by day, then changed from one white outfit into another and worked as an orderly in the hospital at night. One night he had to wheel a patient into surgery. The poor woman looked up from the trolley, saw the student and screamed, 'Help ... it's my butcher!'

Optician

I broke my glasses when I dropped them. I said to the optician, 'Will I have to be examined all over again?' He said, 'No, just your eyes!'

P is for Policeman

Palladium

I'll never forget when I was playing the Palladium ... I drew a line a mile long, but the manager made me go out and erase it!

Parking

I read the other day that only three out of ten murderers get caught. But if you park in the wrong place nine out of ten people get caught. In other words, I reckon it's safer to kill somebody!

One day the wife came home late and said she'd parked the car in Oxford Street. I said, 'Why didn't you park nearer the house?' She said, 'It was so dark over there, I couldn't find all the parts!'

I discovered a great way to avoid getting parking tickets ... remove your windscreen wiper!

The parking situation is getting so bad some guys are carrying bicycles in their cars to get to and from the parking places!

They haven't finished installing all the parking meters around town ... the truck that carries them can't find a place to park!

I bought a raffle ticket the other day. The second prize is a car. The first prize is a parking space!

Parrots

A sailor went to an auction sale where they were selling lots of pets. This magnificent parrot came under the hammer. The sailor started the bidding with ten pounds. Another bidder raised it to twenty-five, but the

A B C D E F G H I J K L M N O P Q R S T U V W X Y Z

sailor was determined to have this parrot and bid thirty. The other bidder came back with thirty-five and the sailor upped the bid to fifty. This went on and on for some time, but the sailor was determined to have the parrot and he finally won the lot. He settled up with the auctioneer and said, 'I paid a lot of money for this bird. Are you sure it can talk?' The cashier said, 'Can he talk? Who do you think was bidding against you?'

An old lady bought a parrot and all the parrot could say was, 'Who is it?' No matter what you asked the parrot, that's all he knew. 'Who is it? Who is it?' One day the plumber came to the door and knocked and the parrot yelled, 'Who is it?' He said, 'It's the plumber.' The parrot kept asking, 'Who is it? Who is it?' and the plumber kept answering back, 'It's the plumber. It's the plumber.' In the end he got so exhausted he fainted on the front porch. A crowd gathered and one of them said, 'Who is it?' The parrot yelled, 'It's the plumber!'

Parties

I was at a party with so many famous people, I was the only one there I'd never heard of!

I was at a party the other night. My wife said, 'Stop saying, "One more for the road." We live here!'

Photography

Two photographers were comparing notes at the end of the day. One said, 'I saw a very sad sight this morning. I was standing on Waterloo Bridge when an old man came up to me and asked me for money. He was trembling with cold, his clothes were threadbare and he hadn't eaten for days. My heart went out to him.' The other said, 'What did you give him?' He said, 'A thousandth of a second at focus 3 point 5!'

Plumber

The plumber asked the woman, 'Where's the drip?' She said, 'He's in the bathroom trying to fix the leak!'

Policemen

This guy walked up to me the other night and said, 'Quick! Did you see a policeman around here?' I said, 'No.' He said, 'Good! Stick 'em up!'

This fellow walked into a police station and asked to see the man who'd been arrested for breaking into his house the night before. The sergeant said, 'And why would you want to do that?' He said, 'So I can find out how he got into my house without waking my wife ... I've been trying to do that for twenty years!'

A policeman stopped a woman for speeding. She said, 'I wasn't doing ninety.' He said, 'I'm going to give you a ticket for trying!'

This officer stopped me and said, 'Why are you driving with a bucket of water on the passenger seat?' I said, 'So that I can dip my headlights!'

O
P

Portrait Painter

This woman went to a portrait painter and said, 'I want you to paint me with my face resting on my hands, showing each finger with a different kind of diamond ring, and on my wrist should be bracelets made of diamonds, rubies, emeralds and pearls, right up to the elbow.' The painter said, 'Did you bring the jewellery with you?' She said, 'Don't be silly. Who said anything about jewellery? It's just that when I die, I want my husband's next wife to go crazy trying to find out where I hid it all!'

This woman was having her portrait painted and after sitting for five hours she turned to the painter and said, 'Well, does it look like me?' He said, 'It looked like you two hours ago! Now I'm trying to improve it!'

Priest

A priest was halfway through his sermon when he saw a man asleep in the front row. He asked the fellow next to him if he would be so kind as to wake him up, but the fellow said, 'I'm sorry, father, but that wouldn't be fair.' The priest said, 'And why not?' The fellow said, 'Well, you put him to sleep ... you wake him up!'

Private Purposes

See Introduction: page 11

Producer

My producer gave me a twenty pound note and told me to get him a sandwich, get something for myself and bring him the change. I came back, gave him the sandwich and fifty pence change. He said, 'That can't be right.' I said, 'You told me to get something for myself, so I bought a shirt and tie!'

Psychiatrists

I spent ten thousand pound on psychiatrists and then found all I needed to solve my problems was ten thousand pounds in the first place!

A woman sent her husband to a psychiatrist because he kept thinking he was a cannibal. When he came back, she said, 'Well, what was he like?' He said, 'Delicious!'

Psychiatrists tell us that one out of every five people is emotionally disturbed. The reason is that the other four are nuts!

I went to my psychiatrist the other day and said, 'Can you cure me of my phobia?' He said, 'What phobia?' I said, 'I can't stand nuts.' He said, 'Neither can I ... get out!'

I told my psychiatrist that I was always having an argument with my wife and it was driving me mad. He said, 'What do you argue about?' I said, 'It's always before going to bed – the cold cream, the facial lotions, the hair curlers.' He said, 'Well, what does she say to you?' I said, 'I don't care what she says. I'm not giving up my facials and my curlers for anyone!'

When I was a kid I went to a psychiatrist for one of those aptitude tests. On the desk he put a pitchfork, a wrench and a hammer and he said to the nurse, 'If he grabs the pitchfork he'll become a farmer. If he grabs the wrench he'll be a mechanic and if he takes the hammer he'll be a carpenter.' I grabbed the nurse!

A woman went to a psychiatrist and said, 'I'm worried about my husband. He thinks he's a washing machine. He keeps rolling his head around and around, back and forth, around and around, and soap and hot water keep coming out of his ears.' He said, 'Oh, I don't think that's anything to worry about.' She said, 'But, doctor, he isn't getting the sheets clean!'

I met a psychiatrist who's a real specialist. He only treats hikers, hunters and campers. Instead of a couch he uses a sleeping bag!

O
P

A woman went to a psychiatrist and complained her husband was always putting an egg in his milk shake. He said, 'So what's wrong with that? Lots of people mix an egg with their milk shake.' She said, 'A fried egg?'

The psychiatrist told me I could consider myself cured. I said, 'Are you kidding? Before I came to you I was Napoleon. Now I'm just another nobody!'

The psychiatrist said, 'What makes you nervous?' I said, 'All day long I'm hearing voices and I don't know where they're coming from.' He said, 'How often does this happen?' I said, 'Whenever I answer the phone!'

What happens when the human body is immersed in water?

The telephone rings!

Q is for Question

Quarrel

My wife's a magician ... she can turn anything into an argument!

I said to my wife, 'I've been thinking it over since this quarrel started and I have to say that everything you said was right.' She said, 'It's too late ... I've changed my mind!'

You can't hear an angry word from the couple next door ... their house is soundproof!

The judge said, 'What started the trouble between you and the plaintiff?' The defendant said, 'Well, it was like this, your honour. He threw a cup of hot coffee over me, I hit him in the face with my bag of tools, then he broke a chair over my head, and the next thing we knew we were quarrelling!'

Questions & Answers

What have you been doing?
This and that.
When?
Now and then.
And where have you been doing it?
Here and there!

When a woman marries a man, why does she take his name?
Why not? She takes everything else he's got!

Quiz Show

I won my wife in a quiz show. She had on a white dress. I thought she was a refrigerator!

The quizmaster said, 'What's the first thing you'll do with the money you've won?' I said, 'I'll count it!'

I read that one guy lost 64,000 pounds in a quiz ... the income tax men were doing the quizzing!

R is for Religion

Rain

Rain is quite wonderful. It makes the flowers grow. It also makes cabs disappear!

The good thing about rain is that you don't have to shovel it!

I never mind the rain, but I get nervous when my next door neighbour starts collecting animals two by two.

It rained so hard, people were jumping into the river to keep from drowning!

Religion

My wife is so religious we can't get any fire insurance. There are too many candles in the house.

I used to be an atheist, but I gave it up ... no holidays!

He's a very religious guy ... he worships money!

A guy asked me if I was a Jehovah's Witness. I said, 'I didn't even see the accident!'

Remarks (heard on planes)

Height never bothers me ... it's the space between me and the ground that gets me nervous!

Who cares what time we land so long as it's on wheels!

I'm not nervous ... my lip always bleeds when I bite it!

What do they mean? We'll have to lighten the load!

Can I open my eyes now?

Restaurants

I said, 'Does the orchestra play anything on request?' The waiter said, 'Yes, sir ... is there anything you would like them to play?' I said, 'Tell them to play dominoes until I've finished eating!'

Three fellows were sitting in a restaurant. The first one told the waiter to bring him a steak ... thick and rare. The second one said, 'I'll have one too, but make it thicker and rarer.' The third one said, 'Just bring the bull out here and I'll bite it as it goes by!'

Three guys went into a restaurant for a cup of tea. One wanted his very hot, the second wanted his very strong and the third said, 'Waiter, just be sure the cup is clean.' The waiter came back with the three cups of tea and said, 'Who asked for the clean cup?'

A man walked into a restaurant, sat down, ate all the rolls on the table and washed them down with water. The waiter came over and said, 'Would you like to order now, sir?' He said 'No, I'm just waiting for a friend.' This went on every day for several days. He came in, sat at the table, ate the rolls, drank the water and told the waiter he was waiting for a friend. On the sixth day he walked in, but there were no rolls on the table. He called the waiter over and said, 'What happened? Where are the rolls?' The waiter said, 'Your friend just left!'

I went into a restaurant to order some roast beef. The waiter said, 'Take the chicken pie instead.' I said, 'I don't like chicken pie. Give me the roast beef.' The waiter said, 'Take the chicken pie.' I said, 'But I don't want chicken pie. Let me talk to the head waiter.' The head waiter came over and said, 'What can I do for you, sir?' and I said, 'I'd like some roast beef.' And the head waiter said, 'Take the chicken pie instead.' I said, 'Damn it, I don't want chicken pie. I want roast beef. Let me talk to the manager!' So the manager came over and said, 'May I help you, sir?' and I said, 'Yes. I asked the waiter for roast beef and he insisted I take the chicken pie instead. I asked the head waiter for roast beef and he tried to make me eat chicken pie. Now I'm asking you, may I have the roast beef?' The manager turned to the head waiter and said, 'Throw this idiot out. He didn't come here to eat, he just came to argue!'

The portions they give you now are ridiculous. The other day a waiter came up and said, 'How did you find the steak?' I said, 'Oh, it was easy. I just lifted up a pea and there it was!'

I was in Paris with my wife and we were in this restaurant. Eventually I grabbed the waiter and said, 'Look here, garçon, my wife and I have been waiting to be served for over an hour. Will you please bring us a bottle of your best champagne?' He said, 'Oui, Monsieur. What year?' I said, 'Right now!'

I said to this Chinese waiter, 'Tell me something. Are there any Chinese Jews?' He said, 'I don't know. I'll go and find out.' So he went and he came back. He said, 'Sorry. There's only apple juice, orange juice and pineapple juice!'

I said, 'Have you got a game pie?' The waiter said, 'We certainly have ... it's fought its way out of the oven twice!'

Show me a man who comes home in the evening and is greeted with a smile, encouraged to take off his shoes, has pillows arranged all around him on the floor and is then served a delicious meal, and I'll show you a man who lives in a Japanese restaurant!

The food was on the table ... but I insisted on plates!

I said to the waiter, 'I'd like to send my compliments to the chef. It's the first time I've ever been served roast beef, ice cream and coffee all at the same temperature!'

Riddles

I said, 'What has four legs, howls at the moon and is full of cement?' He said, 'A coyote.' I said, 'That's right. You're the first one to guess it.' He said, 'But what's with the cement?' I said, 'I just put that in to make it harder!'

Risqué

An eighty-year-old man married a twenty-year-old girl. One of his friends said, 'Let me give you some advice. If you want a happy marriage, take in a lodger.' A few months later they met up again. The friend said, 'How are things working out?' He said, 'They couldn't be better and I owe it all to your advice. What is more, my wife is pregnant.' The friend said, 'And how is the lodger?' He said, 'Oh, she's pregnant too!'

I saw an ad in the paper that read, 'For sale — valuable spot in the country with beautiful view overlooking nudist colony. Reason for moving — failing eyesight!'

This little boy was getting into a lot of trouble at school. His teacher told his mother he was annoying all the little girls and the mother said, 'Just like his father.' Then the teacher said, 'And he gets the little girls in a corner and hugs them and kisses them.' The mother said, 'Yes! Just like his father.' The teacher went on, 'In fact, he never leaves the girls alone ... he's after them all the time.' The mother said, 'Just like his father ... it's a good thing I didn't marry him!'

A woman called her butler into her bedroom and said, 'James, take off my dress. Now take off my slip and my brassiere. Now take off my stockings. Now don't ever let me catch you wearing my clothes again!'

I had a terrible dream the other night. I dreamt I was shipwrecked on a desert island with Jayne Mansfield and Diana Dors. That might not sound so bad, but I was Ava Gardner!

A young girl came to a fancy dress party without any clothes on. The fellow at the door said, 'I'm sorry, miss, but this is a fancy dress party. You're supposed to be in costume and represent something.' So she left and came back later, still in the nude, but this time she was wearing a pair of black shoes and black gloves. The doorman said, 'And what are you supposed to represent?' She said, 'The five of spades!'

When I go out with my girl friend in the evening, she always wears an evening gown. When we go swimming, she wears a swimsuit and when we play tennis, she wears a tennis outfit. Now she won't talk to me. Just because I told her I was coming over to see her on her birthday!

A man went to court for a divorce. The judge asked him why he wanted a divorce and he said, 'Because my wife called me an idiot.' The judge said, 'That's hardly grounds for divorce. Why did she call you an idiot?' I said, 'Well, I came home early one day and caught her making love to another man, so I said, "Hey, what's going on here?" and she said, "Idiot!"'

A little girl was telling her kindergarten teacher, 'Me slept with daddy last night.' The teacher said, 'No, Mary, that's wrong. I slept with daddy last night.' The little girl said, 'Well then, you must have come in after I went to sleep.'

Q
R

Robbery

My neighbour called me the other day and said, 'Are you watching TV?' I said, 'No.' He said, 'I'm not surprised. A guy just came through your kitchen window carrying it!'

Romance

She said, 'Take me in your arms and whisper something soft and sweet.' I said, 'Chocolate fudge!'

S is for Scout

Savings

Every day for two years I've been putting something aside for a rainy day, but what am I going to do with 500 umbrellas and 200 pairs of wellingtons?

Saw

He said, 'What kind of tricks do you do?' I said, 'You've heard of sawing a woman in half?' He said, 'Yes, but that trick's been around for years.' I said, 'Lengthwise?'

Scout

The scoutmaster asked three boy scouts if they had done their good deed for the day. They said, 'Yes, we helped an old lady across the road.' He said, 'Did it take all three of you to do that?' They said, 'Yes! She didn't want to go!'

Shakespeare

I've only read two of Shakespeare's plays – Romeo and Juliet!

I said, 'I've just written a play called *Hamlet*.' He said, '*Hamlet*? But Shakespeare wrote that hundreds of years ago.' I said, 'That's funny. They said the same when I wrote *Othello*!'

Shoes

My wife complained that her feet hurt. I said, 'You've got your shoes on the wrong feet.' She said, 'But these are the only feet I've got.'

I asked the manager if he had any loafers. He said, 'Just a minute and I'll get one of them to serve you!'

I saw an old tramp walking down the street wearing one shoe. I said, 'Hey, you lost your shoe.' He said, 'No, I found one!'

These shoes are killing me. They're so tight, my big toe and my little toe are now going steady!

Shopping

I went into a hardware store and asked the girl to show me some cheap skates. She said, 'I'm sorry, but both the owners are in Florida!'

I wanted to buy her some alligator shoes for her birthday, but I didn't know what size her alligator wore!

I went window shopping ... I couldn't find a window my size!

It isn't the wolf at the door that keeps some husbands broke. It's the mink in the window!

The other day my wife went down to the corner market ... she bought three corners!

I said, 'Do you stock sealing wax?' The girl said, 'I know we have floor wax, but I don't think we've anything for waxing a ceiling!'

I was out all morning trying to get something for my wife ... and I couldn't get a single offer!

I went into this shop and said, 'Have you got a couple of nice steaks?' The guy behind the counter said, 'A couple of nice steaks?' I said, 'Yes – are they rare?' He said, 'Rare? In here they're impossible! You're in the chemist's!'

A cannibal went into a butcher's shop. He said, 'I'll have a pound and a half of Kate and Sidney!'

Two shopkeepers were discussing the drop in business. One said, 'Here it is ... June already and business is terrible.' The other said, 'Well, it's always this way before Christmas!'

Show Business

I've got show business in my blood ... I was bitten by an actor!

I got into show business because I couldn't find my regular line of work ... I'm a shepherd!

One day a guy came up to me and said, 'Hey, Mr Cooper, I want you to know that you're number one on my hit parade' ... so he hit me!

Shyness

I'm so shy, I can't take a bath unless I blindfold my rubber duck!

Singing

I've been taking singing lessons through the mail. I'll admit they haven't helped, but my postman sings like Sinatra!

Lots of people have said I have a voice like Caruso ... Robinson Caruso!

When I sing, I sing with my heart and soul. I'll even sound better when I start using my voice!

When I sing, I cry. I cry because I can't sing!

(sung) He flew through the air with the greatest of ease ...
(spoken) ... he forgot his trapeze!

Sleep

Last night I slept like a log. I woke up in the fireplace!

I sleep like a baby. Every morning I wake up screaming around two!

I am so tired ... I don't know why. I had eight hours sleep last night. I think I must have slept slower than usual!

I worried that as soon as I get into bed I'll drop off ... I'd better order a bigger bed!

Smoking

I got a beautiful smoking jacket for Christmas, but no matter how hard I stuff it into my pipe the sleeves still hang out!

I'm worried about my uncle ... he chews tobacco and then blows smoke rings!

The first time my wife saw me cut off the end of a cigar she said, 'Why don't you buy them the right size?'

This fellow said, 'I get dizzy spells from cigarettes.' I said, 'From inhaling them?' He said, 'No – from bending down to pick them up!'

S
T

My doctor told me to stay
away from cigarettes and to
try chocolate bars instead.
I did, but I had trouble keeping
them alight.

I said to the doctor, 'I'm worried
about my wife smoking.' He said,
'But a lot of women smoke.'
I said, 'I know, but she inhales.'
He said, 'That's alright. A lot of
women who smoke inhale.' I said,
'But she never exhales!'

If you want to stop smoking,
carry wet matches!

Snooker

Did you hear about the snooker player who had a nervous breakdown?
Every time he leaned over the table he got the shakes. His doctor
prescribed a long rest!

Spring

Spring must be here ... this morning I heard the first robin coughing its
little brains out!

Stardom

What a reception I got when I stepped off the plane. Everybody started
shouting, 'There's Tony Curtis! There's Tony Curtis!' So I turned around
and there was Tony Curtis!

Strikes

Two guys were in a picket line. One of them said, 'Do you know what it's all about?' The other said, 'We're striking for shorter hours.' The other one said, 'I'm in favour of that. I always thought sixty minutes was too long!'

During the transport strike I saw an old lady standing by the side of the road and decided to give her a lift. After several miles I turned to her and said, 'Madam, where shall I let you out?' She said, 'Thank you, but I didn't want to say anything to hurt your feelings. I was going the other way!'

Superstition

I'm so superstitious, I wouldn't walk under a black cat!

Swimming

I tried to swim the Channel once, but I used too much grease. I kept slipping out of the water!

They always say start at the bottom if you want to learn something ... but suppose you want to learn to swim?

S
T

A lifeguard on the beach heard a man yelling for help. He shouted, 'Help! I can't swim. I've got my hands in my pockets. Help!' The lifeguard picked up his megaphone and yelled back, 'Take your hands out of your pockets!' The man yelled back, 'What ... and let the water in?'

They've got a big sign that says, 'No Smoking In The Pool.' Are they afraid the water will catch fire?

T is for Tap

Tap

My little boy ... no one could do anything with him. His teacher said, 'What's the answer to water on the brain?' He said, 'A tap on the head!'

Tattoos

This tattooist wanted to draw a great big eagle right across his back. He always wanted to do it ... draw a great big eagle with a wing on each shoulder and its talons in the small of his back. For twenty years he wanted to do it, but he was so busy he couldn't get round to it!

Taxis

The taxi driver said, 'I'll charge two pounds each for you and your wife. The kids can ride for free.' The father turned to the kids and said, 'Okay. Jump in, children, and have a nice ride. Your mother and I will see you back at the hotel!'

I said to the driver, 'Can't you go any faster?' He said, 'I sure can, but I'm not allowed to leave the cab!'

A cab driver turned to his passenger and said, 'I couldn't help noticing that hearing aid you're wearing. Do you mind it much?' The passenger said, 'Not at all. As a matter of fact, nearly all of us have some physical weakness.' The driver said, 'You're right. Look at me. I can hardly see a foot in front of me!'

I know a cab driver who weighs 200 lbs, is six feet tall, chews tobacco and loves to fight. Even her husband is afraid of her!

Teeth

I could tell she had false teeth ... it came out in conversation!

Forgive me if I speak slowly ... I lost my bridge on the River Kwai!

Telephone

My wife answered the phone, said, 'Yes, that's right,' and put it down again. I said, 'Who was that?' She said, 'It's some woman who keeps saying "Long distance from America"!'

One thing worries me ... why aren't wrong numbers ever busy?

Television

My wife watches so many medical shows, I can only talk to her during visiting hours!

I'm in favour of pay television ... if they pay me, I'll watch anything!

Television has opened up a whole new field of unemployment for me!

I always had trouble getting on television. I even offered to kill myself on TV. It would be a real first!

Thoughts for the Day

I now leave you with a thought for the day ...

Everybody makes mistakes. An architect covers his mistakes with ivy, a doctor covers his mistakes with earth and a chef covers his mistakes with mayonnaise!

Show me a man who lost all his money and can still laugh and I'll show you an idiot!

You haven't a real hangover until you can't stand the noise made by Alka Seltzer!

As my father used to say, 'Never cry over spilt milk ... it could have been whiskey!'

Love your enemies ... it'll drive them nuts!

A barking dog never whistles!

My mind keeps saying I shouldn't drink and have anything to do with women. The rest of me says, 'Who asked you?'

Why is it you always see a parking space when you haven't got a car?

In the words of that great philosopher, 'A friend in need is a pest!'

If I had to live my life all over again ... I wouldn't have the strength!

When you lend a friend ten pounds and you never see him again ... it's worth it!

S
T

Where did mothers learn all those things they tell their daughters not to do?

There's only one thing to give a man who has everything ... penicillin!

You can lead a horse to water, but teach him to lie on his back and float and you've got something!

Things always turn out right in the end. I knew an old man who was unlucky all his life. Then when they were digging his grave they struck oil.

Never tell people your troubles. Half of them are not interested and the other half are glad you're getting what's coming to you!

And never worry about getting older. Just remember that when you stop getting older, you're dead!

Tips

To show my appreciation I gave the decorator an extra ten pounds and told him to take the missus to the movies. That night he was back wearing his best clothes. I said, 'What's the matter? Did you forget something?' He said, 'No, I just came back to take the missus to the movies.'

Town

As Fred Allen said, the town was so dull one day the tide went out and it never came back!

Traffic

The traffic is so bad. One day I was offered a lift and said, 'No thanks ... I'm in a hurry!'

Tramp

A tramp asked me if I could give him something for a cup of coffee ... so I gave him a lump of sugar!

Transport

I feel travel sick. I just got off a train and had to ride backwards all the way. Someone said, 'Why didn't you ask somebody sitting opposite to change seats with you?' I said, 'I would have, but I was all alone in the carriage!''

A man was standing next to me on the bus when he tapped me on the shoulder. He said, 'Are you getting off soon?' I said, 'No. Why?' He said, 'You're standing on my foot!'

Travel

I've been to Paris so many times I'm beginning to feel like a parasite!

We went to Switzerland and there was this beautiful mountain. I said to the guide, 'There must be romantic stories about it.' He said, 'Yes. One day two lovers climbed to the top and they were never seen again.' I said, 'What happened?' He said, 'They went down the other side!'

I took my wife on a cruise and she threw the laundry out of the porthole. She thought it was a washing machine.

When I was in Paris I spent two days in my room trying to learn enough French to get downstairs!

Tunnel

The British and the French were discussing the Channel Tunnel. The chief engineer said, 'The idea is that we'll send a thousand men in one end and a thousand men in the other end and they'll meet halfway.' Someone said, 'But suppose they don't meet.' The engineer said, 'Then we'll have two tunnels!'

S
T

U is for Umbrella

Ugly

In school I had to stand with my face to the wall ... not because I was bad, but because I was ugly!

She was so ugly, she kept sending her mirror back for repairs!

She was too ugly to have her face lifted, so they lowered her body instead!

Umbrella

Let a smile be your umbrella ... and you'll get soaking wet!

Yesterday I saw five men standing under a single umbrella and not one of them got a drop of water on him. It wasn't raining!

Undertakers

Never trust an undertaker ... he'll always let you down!

I said, 'You told me your son was a doctor.' He said, 'No I didn't ... I said he followed the medical profession!'

This undertaker was complaining about business. He said, 'I haven't buried a living soul for three months!'

This fellow phoned an undertaker to sort out his wife's funeral. The undertaker said, 'Your wife? Didn't I bury her two years ago?' He said, 'I married again.' The undertaker said, 'Congratulations!'

This girl started to date an undertaker. Her friend said, 'You should be careful. He may be after you for your body!'

V is for Ventriloquist

Value

There's an easy way of finding out the value of money ... try to borrow some!

Vegetables

Every day this guy came into a bar with a potato stuck in his ear. Then one day he showed up with a stick of celery in his ear instead. The barman said, 'Why the change?' He said, 'The doctor told me to cut out fattening foods!'

Vegetarian

My little boy bit into an apple, saw a worm and said, 'From now on I'll think I'll be a vegetarian!'

Ventriloquists

This ventriloquist fell on hard times and was forced to take work as the accomplice of a phoney medium. At one séance he was pretending to be Mr Smith, whose widow had paid fifty pounds for the privilege. After talking to her husband for a long time, she said, 'I can't believe I could talk to my husband for just fifty pounds.' The ventriloquist said, 'Well, for a hundred you could talk to him while he's drinking a glass of water!'

This fellow walked into a bar with a chicken under one arm and a crocodile under the other. The barman said, 'What'll you have?' He said, 'A whiskey and soda.' Then the crocodile spoke up and said, 'I'll have a gin and tonic.' The barman said, 'That's amazing. I've never seen a crocodile that could talk before.' He said, 'He can't. The chicken's a ventriloquist!'

Violin

I play the violin just like Menuhin ... under the chin!

W is for Wand

Waiters

A waiter is a man who believes that money grows on trays!

One day a waiter fell sick and was rushed to hospital. He was lying on the table in great pain when a doctor passed by. He said, 'Hey doctor, can't you do something for me?' The doctor said, 'I'm sorry. This isn't my table!'

The waiters at my hotel ... they're so sentimental. One of them held out his hand and said, 'I hope you're not going to forget me.' I shook his hand and said, 'Of course not. I'll write every day!'

I went into a restaurant and waited an hour to be served. Eventually I grabbed a waiter and said, 'How about something to eat?' He said, 'Who's got time to sit down?'

I said to the waiter, 'There's a fly in my soup.' He said, 'I know ... the chef used to be a tailor!'

I said, 'Do you serve shepherd's pie?' He said, 'Of course, as long as they leave their sheep outside!'

I said to the waiter, 'Hey, what kind of duck is this? It tastes like fish.' He said, 'I know. It's haddock!'

I found a fly in my soup and said to the waiter, 'What's the meaning of this?' He said, 'How should I know. I'm a waiter, not a fortune teller!'

I said to the waiter, 'There's a fly in my ice cream.' He said, 'Serves him right ... let him freeze to death. This morning he was in the soup!'

The waiter gave me a menu. It had everything on it, so I asked for a clean one!

I said to the waiter, 'A piece of plaster just fell in my soup.' He said, 'Well, as long as you're paying ceiling prices, you're entitled to a piece of the ceiling!'

This fellow had rice in his hair. I said, 'Did you get married today?' He said, 'No, I had a fight with a Chinese waiter!'

I said, 'Waiter, this chicken's got one leg shorter than the other.' He said, 'What do you want to do? Eat it or dance with it?'

Last night I ordered a whole meal in French. The waiter was surprised. It was a Chinese restaurant!

The waiter brought me everything but a spoon. I said, 'This coffee is too hot for me to stir with my finger!' He brought me another cup and said, 'This one's a lot cooler!'

I said to the waiter, 'There's no chicken in this chicken soup.' He said, 'And there's no horse in the horseradish either!'

When I go to a restaurant I like my food hot. So I told the waiter I wanted my soup real hot. I said, 'I mean it should be real boiling hot. In fact, if you can carry it, don't bother bringing it because it won't be hot enough!'

A cannibal boarded a cruise ship and went to the dining room. The waiter said, 'Menu, sir?' He said, 'No, the passenger list!'

I said to the waiter, 'How do you get a glass of water in this place?' He said, 'I don't know ... how about setting yourself on fire?'

I said, 'How long will my spaghetti be?' The waiter said, 'I don't know ... we never measure it!'

He said, 'Do you want red or white?' I said, 'I don't mind. I'm colour-blind.'

I thought I'd start a conversation, so I said to the waiter, 'It looks like rain.' He said, 'I know, but it's soup!'

Wand

Here's a magic wand ... there's a white tip there and a white tip there ... now the reason for the white tips is to separate the ends from the centre!

Weather

It was so cold, my teeth were chattering so much, I couldn't put them back in my mouth!

It was so cold, my teeth were chattering so much, they broke the glass I keep them in!

It was so cold, my teeth were chattering so much, I took them out and went to bed!

It was so cold, I opened my wardrobe door and my best suit was wearing my overcoat!

I went to Margate for my holidays. It was so cold. There was a guy shivering on the beach in a bathing suit. He was purple all over. I said, 'You can't expect to get a tan in this weather.' He said, 'Well, I'm going home with some colour and I don't care what colour it is!'

There was a guy sitting there holding a piece of rope up in the air. I said, 'What's that for?' He said, 'This is a weather gauge.' I said, 'How can you predict the weather with a piece of rope?' He said, 'It's easy. When the rope swings back and forth, it's windy and when it gets wet, it's raining!'

It was ninety in the shade. I'm no fool – I stayed in the sun!

Weddings

The other day I went to a wedding and I never saw two happier people. Not the bride and groom – her parents!

Was the bride jealous! She was the only bride who ever had a male bridesmaid!

A wedding is a funeral where you smell your own flowers!

I'll never forget our wedding. Her mother cried and her father cried. I never saw two people cry so much. No wonder ... it cost a fortune!

The trouble with being best man at a wedding ... you never get a chance to prove it!

I had a brass band at our wedding. I put it on my wife's finger!

Well Dressed

See Introduction: page 11

What If?

What if William Tell had been nearsighted?

What if Abraham Lincoln had waited to see it on TV?

What if Lady Godiva had had a crew cut?

Wives

I asked my wife to marry me and be the mother of my children. She said, 'How many have you got?'

I'll never forget the first time I took her home to meet my mother. I said, 'This girl is just wonderful. She loves to cook. She loves to sew. She takes care of the house and does everything.' My mother said, 'That's good. I'll use her on Tuesdays and Thursdays!'

When I first met my wife, every morning I tried to bring her breakfast in bed. It wasn't easy ... she lived at the YWCA.

My wife and I never quarrel. You know why? I'm a coward!

I gave my wife a ring on her birthday. I reversed the charges!

My wife and I were having lunch together and she said, 'Would you pass me over the mustard!' So I did ... she wasn't half heavy!

I'm a little worried about her tonight. This morning she left home at nine o'clock and she isn't back yet. I don't know what to think. She may have gone shopping or she may have been in an accident or kidnapped or even murdered. Gee, I hope she isn't shopping!

I don't like to talk about my wife behind her back. I only do it because it's safer that way!

I'm not knocking my wife. She is kind and considerate and really too good for me. If only she'd realise this and leave me!

She's such a terrible cook, for ten years she thought poached eggs were illegal!

My wife had a bad habit of biting her nails, but I cured her. I hid her teeth!

I bought my wife a mink stole and now I'm up to her neck in debt!

I'm the boss in my family. Every night when I get home my wife brings me my slippers, my pipe and my apron!

My wife said, 'Why don't you buy me a mink coat? I'm always cold.' I said, 'That's why!'

My wife's a lovely mover ... she works for Pickfords!

The other night I had an argument with my wife in the launderette ... but we went home and ironed things out!

My wife is the kind of wife who when she has a bad night wakes her husband and says, 'What's the matter? Can't you sleep either?'

My wife is one of those women who always enters a room voice first!

She's got me where I eat out of her hand ... saves a lot of dishwashing!

I've got a wife who never misses me. Her aim is perfect!

My wife decided to knit me a pair of socks. They're fine, but just a little snug under the arms!

I found a way to cure my wife from falling out of bed. I make her sleep on the floor!

She is always complaining about headaches, but it's her own fault. I keep telling her – if she's going to jump out of bed, she should do it feet first!

I can't stand my wife smoking in bed. I know a lot of women smoke in bed, but face down?

I said to my wife, 'Let's go out tonight and have some fun.' She said, 'Okay, but leave the hall light on if you get in before me!'

One day I came home and found a big cake with seven candles on it. I said, 'Whose birthday is it?' She said, 'That's for the dress I'm wearing ... it's seven years old today!'

Actually I take my wife everywhere, but she keeps coming back!

I met my wife at a dance ... I thought she was at home with the kids!

W
X

My wife dislocated her jaw and couldn't talk. So I phoned the doctor and told him to drop round anytime in a few weeks or a month!

My wife and I used to have such fun at the beach. First she would bury me in the sand, then I would bury her in the sand. One of these days I'm going to go back and dig her up!

I took my wife out to lunch. Halfway through the meal she fainted. The waiter rushed up and said, 'Do you want a stretcher?' I said, 'No, thank you. She's long enough as she is!'

She keeps asking me for something to drive. So I bought her a hammer and a packet of nails!

Everything Sophia Loren wears my wife goes out and buys. The other day she bought a pair of those Italian sandals and now she looks just like her ... from the ankles down!

Take away Sophia Loren's sexy look and take away her figure and what have you got? My wife!

She's the best little wife a guy ever had ... even if her husband doesn't think so!

They say a woman's work is never done and my wife's cooking proves it!

My wife is the fussiest housekeeper you ever saw. She even puts a newspaper under the cuckoo clock!

She's always complaining about clothes. The other day she said, 'Just look at me. My clothes are so shabby. If anyone came to the door they'd think I was the cook.' I said, 'Not if they stayed to dinner!'

She has been trying to keep up with the Joneses for years and we finally made it. We now owe as much money as they do!

She always serves me food that melts in the mouth, but how many ice cubes can a man swallow?

Actually she bakes wonderfully – on the beach!

You know why I call her 'Dear' ... she's got antlers sticking out of her head!

There's only one place I go when I want to get away from her. I hide in the kitchen!

She cooks so bad, the cat has only three lives left!

The other day I asked her when she was going to straighten up the house. She said, 'Why? Is it tilted?'

One day I asked her why my shaving brush was as stiff as a board. She said, 'I don't know ... it felt soft yesterday, when I was painting the birdcage!'

She's the kind of wife – when she can't find any hairs on your coat, she accuses you of running around with a bald-headed woman!

I said, 'Why do you wear your wedding ring on the wrong finger?' She said, 'Because I married the wrong guy!'

She just got her driver's licence. Now all her accidents will be legal. What she doesn't know about driving a car would fill a hospital!

To give you an idea of how my wife drives, the other day she almost killed me backing out of the garage. She said, 'Thank goodness it was only you. It might have been a stranger!'

I won't say what kind of driver she is, but once she was hit by a house!

She once got a speeding ticket going through the car wash!

Once she left the garage at fifty miles an hour and then came back ... she forgot the car!

One day my wife came home with the car a total wreck. I said, 'What happened?' She said, 'Well, it was either run into this other car or else have an accident!'

When she was brought into court, the judge said it was the worst case of hit-and-run he had ever seen. He thought she was the victim!

I don't know what to buy my wife for her birthday. I don't know whether to buy her a box of chocolates, a diamond ring, a fur coat or a new car. That's what I'll get her ... a box of chocolates.

I asked the girl behind the counter what can I get for my wife? She said, 'I don't know. What are you asking for her?'

My wife is always telling me that women are like wine ... the older they get, the better they become. So I locked her in the cellar!

At least when she drives, people are safe on the street ... she drives on the pavement!

I said to my wife, 'Why don't you stop at red lights?' She said, 'Once you've seen one, you've seen them all!'

My wife phoned. She said, 'There's water in the carburettor.' I said, 'Where's the car?' She said, 'In the lake!'

My wife ran away with the gardener. Isn't that awful? Good gardeners are hard to find!

After we were married she told me she would cook and darn all my socks. I said, 'That won't be necessary ... just darn them!'

My wife is a magician. Yesterday she turned our car into a tree!

My wife's got a heart of gold ... hard and yellow!

My wife's a light eater ... as soon as it gets light she starts eating!

My wife couldn't close her eyes all night. She put her eyelashes on backwards!

She said, 'Do you like my hair in a bun?' I said, 'I wouldn't care if you wore it in a loaf of bread!'

My wife does great bird impressions – she watches me like a hawk!

I said, 'But if you saw someone stealing our car, why didn't you scream or something?' She said, 'Don't worry. I wrote down the registration number before he got out of sight!'

The other day my wife asked me for fifty pounds. I said, 'Money, money, money ... that's all you ever ask me for is money! You need brains instead of money.' She said, 'Maybe, but I just thought I'd ask you for what you had the most of!'

She never argues. She just tells me I'm wrong and lets it go at that.

Mind you – I always get the last word. I apologise!

Women

When meeting a beautiful girl an Englishman raises an eyebrow, a Frenchman kisses her hand, an American asks for her phone number and a Russian cables the Kremlin for instructions!

She's the kind of woman, if she can't say anything good about another woman, she loves it!

She was so beautiful, when I took her home in a taxi, I could hardly keep my eyes on the meter!

I'm fussy what kind of girl I go out with ... they've got to have shoes!

She was wearing a living bra ... and it bit her!

She's a Cinderella girl ... at the stroke of twelve, she passes out!

She's the kind of girl you look at twice. The first time you don't believe it!

Since she left me I can't sleep a wink ... she took the mattress with her!

Worry

I offered a guy a hundred pounds to worry for me. He said, 'Where's the hundred quid?' I said, 'That's your first worry!'

Wrestling

I used to be a wrestler. You know, some wrestlers wear a toga ... some wear a leopard skin ... and some wear fancy robes. Me – I was different. I wore a suit of armour!

I used to be an all-in wrestler. I had to give it up. After the first round I was all in!

FUN-MASTER MONTHLY
"COMEDIAN"

"THE COMEDIAN" for JA
Vol.9 No.6 (102nd iss

M O R E   O N E - L I N E R S (continue

He wasn't bald, his head just grew up through h

My act got a wonderful review--in "POPULAR MECHA

My golf is sure improving. I'm missing the ball
than I used to.

It isn't the line you GIVE a gal that BOTHERS he
PAWS in between!

I don't know where my next dollar's coming from b
already knows where it's going!

She's always making mountains out of moth-balls!

When I was born I was so fat my Mother had to jack
change my diapers! (or: when HE was born, etc.)

I gave my girl a cultured pearl set--a dozen oyste

Boy, was that restaurant expensive! I said to the
"Haven't you got any slightly used steaks?"

Before I leave, I have some advice for you people wh
falling asleep. Drink a pint of rye before you
SLEEP TIGHT!

I got a one-man dog...he only bites ME!

Everytime he gets a raise his wife gets a new hat.
seems to go to HER head!

X is for

X

Have you ever thought ... if you sign something with an 'X', how do you cross it out?

I've invented a new cleaning fluid. It gets rid of all the Xs that mark the spot!

X-Rated

I saw my first X-rated Western the other day. Even the wagons weren't covered!

X-Rays

I gave her an X-ray of my chest. I just wanted to show her my heart was in the right place!

My doctor is an old-fashioned doctor. He doesn't give you an X-ray ... he just holds you up to the light!

A hospital technician got married to a woman who'd come in for an X-ray ... he must have seen something in her!

I said to the consultant, 'My head feels like there are a million little teeny-weeny light bulbs in there.' He said, 'Why don't you have it X-rayed?' I said, 'I did.' He said, 'What did they find?' I said, 'A million little teeny-weeny light bulbs!'

Xylophone

Two dinosaurs walked passed a xylophone. One of them said, 'She's pretty, but she's all skin and bones!'

Y is for Youth

Youth

I'll never forget my first girlfriend. Her father shot at me, her brother threw stones at me and her mother hit me with a broom. I can take a hint!

When I was young I always leaned towards blondes ... but they kept pushing me back!

Youth is the first forty years of your life, but the first twenty of everybody else's!

In the words of Milton Berle, 'We spend the first half of our lives trying to understand the older generation, and the second half trying to understand the younger!'

In other words, if young people were wise, they'd miss half the fun!

Adolescence is when boys begin to notice that girls notice boys who notice girls.

I'll never forget my first sweetheart. I asked her father if I could marry her. Her father said, 'Can you make her happy?' I said, 'Happy? You should have seen her last night in the back of the car!'

It wasn't easy to get us kids to eat olives. I had to start off on martinis!

A woman should hold on to her youth, but not when she's driving!

Z is for Zebra

Zebras

A leopard went to see a psychiatrist. He said, 'Every time I look at my wife I see spots before my eyes.' The psychiatrist said, 'That's only natural.' The leopard said, 'But doctor, she's a zebra!'

A man went to see a psychiatrist. He said, 'It's odd, but I feel that I'm a zebra. Everywhere I look on my body I see black stripes.' The psychiatrist said, 'Take one of these pills every day for a week and it should get rid of the black stripes.' He came back in a few days and said, 'Doctor, I feel great. The black stripes have gone. Have you anything for the white ones?'

The zebra said to the lion, 'Let's switch roles for a while.' The lion said, 'Okay, I'm game!'

Zoo

Two leopards were being fed at the zoo. One sat back and said, 'That hit just the right spot!'

This big elephant and this tiny mouse were in the same cage at the zoo. The elephant was in a really foul mood. He looked down at the mouse and said, 'You are the weakest, puniest, most insignificant creature I've ever seen.' The mouse said, 'But don't forget ... I've been ill!'

I went to the zoo the other day and the zoo-keeper started chasing me because I was feeding the monkeys. I was feeding them to the lions!

This fellow worked at the zoo throwing fish to the pelicans. It wasn't a great job, but it filled the bill!

I took my wife to the zoo, but they wouldn't accept her!

Acknowledgements

This is the third volume of an ongoing series chronicling the life, comedy and methods of one of the greatest comedy talents of all time. Again I thank Tommy's daughter, Vicky Cooper, and John Miles, on behalf of the Tommy Cooper Estate, for their support of this project.

Special acknowledgement is made to Fred Allen, Val Andrews, Eddie Bayliss, Jack Benny, Milton Berle, Martin Breese, Peter Cagney, Gwen Cooper, David Drummond, Pinkie DuFort, Beatrice Ferrie, Miff Ferrie, Colin Fox, Jerome Flynn, the team at FremantleMedia, Eddie Gay, Billy Glason, Tommy Godfrey, Buddy Hackett, Vince Healy, David Hemingway, Peter Hudson, Tudor Jones and the members of the Tommy Cooper Appreciation Society, Henry Lewis, Trevor Lewis, Clive Mantle, Max Miller, Robert Orben, Art Paul, Patrick Ryecart, Freddie Sadler, Stuart Snaith and the team at 2entertain, Eric Sykes, Chris Woodward and Henny Youngman.

Trevor Dolby had the continued conviction that Tommy Cooper could make us laugh again on the printed page and I extend my thanks to him and his team at Preface including Nicola Taplin, Neil Bradford and Phil Brown. While every effort has been made to trace the owners of copyright material produced herein, the publishers would like to apologise for any omissions and will be pleased to incorporate missing acknowledgements in future editions, provided that notification is made to them in writing.

Andy Spence took on the challenge of committing the range and detail of the Cooper joke archive to the printed page. Coupled with my gratitude to him is the wish that my comic hero could have seen the results of his research arranged so accessibly. Equally supportive have been the unstinting enthusiasm of my representative, Charles Armitage, the efficiency of his associate, Di Evans, and of course the loving tolerance of my wife, Sue. I thank them all!

JOHN FISHER

ALSO AVAILABLE ...

THE TOMMY COOPER JOKE BOOK

Put the smile back into life with Tommy's favourite jokes, stories and photographs.

TOMMY COOPER'S MIRTH, MAGIC & MISCHIEF

Relive Tommy's magic with gags galore, terrific tricks and a priceless trip down memory lane along with many previously unpublished photographs.

TOMMY COOPER'S APPLE APP

- Tommy tells you his best gags with the unique Laugh-o-Meter. When you keep laughing, then the jokes keep coming!

- Learn to perform some classic Cooper tricks.

www.tommycooperapps.co.uk

TOMMY COOPER DVD's

- **Tommy Cooper** – The very best of.

- **Cooper's Half Hours** – *The Tommy Cooper Show.*

- **Tommy Cooper Just Like That!** – Magic, mirth and music!

- **The Best Of Tommy Cooper** – This special selection contains some extracts from Cooper at his best including his infamous appearances on *Parkinson* and *The Bob Monkhouse Show.*